Ina Vestal
$^a/250$

D1596790

THE GREAT SECRET

THE GREAT SECRET

by MAURICE MAETERLINCK

NEW FOREWORD BY
LESLIE SHEPARD

UNIVERSITY BOOKS INC.
NEW HYDE PARK, N. Y. 11040

NEW FOREWORD

OF ALL the great questions of religion, philosophy and science, the greatest is the meaning of life itself. Many answers have been given by doctrinaire religions, but only the mystic has known the Great Secret.

This book is a survey of the historical quest for the meaning of life, by a man who was a strange blend of mystic and realist. He was a world-famous playwright, a Nobel prize-winner for literature, once declared to be the Shakespeare of Belgium, yet so much has happened in the modern world nineteen years after his death that today his work is largely overlooked, his plays not revived, and the present book glossed over in biographies. In fact, this is a neglected masterpiece.

If you mention the name of Maurice Maeterlinck today, people may pause, think hard, then say, "Oh yes, isn't he the man who wrote 'The Blue Bird'?" True, it was his most well-known play, a charming symbolic drama cast in a pattern reminiscent of Barrie's "Peter Pan." It was deservedly popular all over the world, and it made a permanent name and fortune for Maeterlinck, but his other works are full of deeper and more subtle wisdom.

Maurice Maeterlinck was an extraordinary paradox—a dreamer who enjoyed amateur boxing, a shy poet and essayist who rode a motorcycle and drove one of the first automobiles, a mystical playwright fond of roller-skating, a literary lion with a taste for good food and wine who kept a submachine gun under his bed to scare away intruders and newspaper reporters. His own life mirrors many of the contradictions of the larger life he describes in this book.

He was born of Flemish ancestors August 29, 1862 at

Ghent, Belgium, and christened *Mauritius Polydorus Maria Bernardus Maeterlinck*. He spent seven years in a Jesuit College at Sainte-Barbe before studying law at Ghent University. Much of his outlook is overshadowed by the severe undertones of his religious training, and the brooding atmosphere of Flanders with the strange effects of light and shade which inspired great painters. When only a young man, his sturdy peasant-like appearance contrasted oddly with his extraordinary shyness and sensitivity, and the split between physical and spiritual life runs all through his later writings.

In 1886 he qualified as a member of the Ghent bar, although his heart was not in the legal profession—rather in the books he read by writers like Plato, Plotinus, Coleridge and Emerson, and especially mystics like Boehme, Novalis, and his own countryman Ruysbroeck. He spent some months in the literary circles of Paris, and in 1889 published a slim volume of poems *Les Serres Chaudes*. In the following year his play *La Princesse Maleine* received an unexpected eulogy from the novelist Octave Mirbeau who wrote a generous review, comparing this unknown young writer with Shakespeare. From this point onwards Maeterlinck abandoned law and followed a literary career.

By 1891 he had published three more plays, and a translation from the Flemish of Ruysbroeck's mystical work *Adornment of Spiritual Marriage*. There followed four more plays, including the superb *La Mort de Tintagiles* (which I have always thought his most beautiful and poignant drama) and a translation from the German of the *Disciples at Saïs* by Novalis. Many of Maeterlinck's plays were concerned with symbolic events and human beings haunted by a mysterious destiny.

In 1895 came his meeting with the actress Georgette Leblanc, sister of popular novelist Maurice Leblanc (creator of detective Arsène Lupin). There ensued one of those ideal passions of which men and women still dream, and which are the inspiration of romantic novelists. After a first meeting, Maeter-linck sent a book inscribed "To Georgette Leblanc, the heroine of great dreams." Because she was formally tied by an earlier contract which could not be dissolved, marriage was out of the question. She became his mistress.

This strange love affair lasted for twenty three years be-fore being cruelly torn apart by conflicting emotions and events.

Georgette Leblanc inspired Maeterlinck. Her thoughts, in-tuitions, and even some of her writings were woven into his own like a tapestry. She acted in his dramas and he wrote plays for her; she negotiated on his behalf where his own hy-persensitivity might have made impossible difficulties. Much of the time they lived in the vast old Benedictine Abbey of Saint-Wandrille, Normandy, where Georgette staged his plays in a natural setting.

Gradually the period of romantic love turned to some-thing like maternal affection, then imperceptibly irritations and misunderstandings arose. They drifted apart, and finally, after years of inspiration and creative companionship their association was shattered in an incoherent tangle of unhappy drama. Some of the story is told in Georgette Leblanc's *Souvenirs* (translated as *Maeterlinck and I*), written years afterwards but with the memory still raw. It is impossible to read this moving story without deep feelings, but of course it tells only her own view of the matter. She wrote it living in a lonely lighthouse on the Normandy coast, midway be-tween sky and sea, with the fantastic setting of sun, wind, storms, and a limitless horizon. It is almost a Maeterlinck play.

Afterwards, in 1919, he married Renée Dahon, a younger woman who as a girl had acted in a production of his play *The Blue Bird* in Paris. Their happiness together endured for the rest of his life.

In the period before the final break with Georgette Le-

vii

blanc, Maeterlinck wrote the collections of essays which were precursors of the present book: *The Treasure of the Humble, Wisdom and Destiny, The Ruined Temple, The Double Garden, Life and Flowers*, and *The Unknown Guest* (a masterly study of psychical phenomena). Another important prose work was *The Life of the Bee*, which drew from his own experience and observations as a beekeeper, presenting the strange drama of the insect world with scientific care and mystical insight. He wrote the plays *Monna Vanna, Joyzelle*, and the famous and popular *The Blue Bird*, which had its world premiere at the Arts Theatre, Moscow in a Stanislavsky production in 1907.

In 1911 Maeterlinck was honored with the Nobel Prize for Literature "on account of his diverse literary activity and especially his dramatic works, which are outstanding for their richness of imagination and for poetic realism . . ."

He had written a strange metaphysical work on Death (*La Mort*), which he revised in 1913 to include large sections on psychical research and Spiritualism. On January 26, 1914 the Catholic Church placed his name on the Index of works contrary to religion and morality. Only a few months later the German armies entered Maeterlinck's Belgium and death swept across Europe into France. Maeterlinck had to leave his home. He tried to enlist, but the 52-year-old author was refused by the authorities and informed that his writings would be more valuable to the cause. He gave lectures and wrote, amongst other things, the powerful propaganda play *The Burgomaster of Stilemonde*.

In the post-war period Maeterlinck travelled widely. He gave a lecture tour in America and even met Sam Goldwyn in Hollywood, who persuaded him to write three film scenarios; apparently nothing came of them. In 1932 the Belgium Government honored Maeterlinck with the title of Count. Some of his important books in the twenties and thirties include the present work, *The Life of the White Ant*, and

Mountain Paths. At the age of 77 he lived quietly with his wife at Nice, but while on a visit to Portugal history repeated itself and Europe was overrun by a second world war. Maeterlinck and his wife salvaged a few possessions and fled to America, virtually penniless. Although he continued to write he was clearly out of touch with a new world, as he expressed it: "Meeting with people whom one does not know, who say things to you that do not interest you, in a language that you do not understand." Many people were kind to him but here, in his advancing years, in a strange country, he was ill at ease. He belonged to an older world that had already passed away.

Towards the end of 1947 he was welcomed back to Europe and took up his residence at Nice once more. After two years in poor health the figure of death that had haunted so much of his life arrived to claim him. He died May 6, 1949, in his 87th year.

In his book of thoughts and aphorisms *The Great Beyond* he had written: "Death is difficult for those who keep her waiting too long." His last words, as poignant as any lines in a play, were whispered to his wife: "I have only one regret, that of leaving you." The London newspaper *The Times* said in an obituary that his influence "has been felt not so much in the schools as in the hearts of people responsive to his suggestions of the inward peace and dignity to be wrested from life in a mechanistic age."

*　*　*

The present work is a mature summary of many years of mystical and philosophical inquiry. With brilliant insight and wide learning Maeterlinck traces the secret doctrine from the religions of ancient India, Egypt, Persia, Chaldea and Greece, through the Gnostics, Neoplatonists. Kabbalists, Alchemists, to modern Occultists and Metapsychists (psychical scientists). In measured penetrating prose he reviews the

ix

whole field of metaphysical inquiry—the insights of mysticism, the beliefs and practices of religion, the imperatives of morality, the strange operations of destiny, and the fundamental bases of occult tradition, Spiritualism and psychical phenomena. Unencumbered by traditional dogmas Maeterlinck moves easily through the tangled history of the world's great religions and cults, discussing those secrets once reserved for a few select initiates.

This book crystallizes the unusual unity of Maeterlinck's understanding and thought, expressed in the range of his literary and dramatic work.

In his early poems he first communicated his sense of the mystery behind the phenomenal world. In his symbolic plays the mystery is enhanced by the dramatic emotions of human beings caught up in an incomprehensible but implacable destiny. In his prose essays he investigated the natural morality behind the world of appearances. He explored not only the strange destinies of human affairs but also the incredible and baffling life of insects and plants, notably in his fine book *The Life of the Bee*, and his essays on "The Intelligence of Flowers" (*Life and Flowers*) and "The Insect World" (*Mountain Paths*). Equally fascinating is his profound understanding of the phenomena of psychical science which he reviewed in *The Unknown Guest* and the present book, citing ghosts, clairvoyance, precognition, materializations, and even the experiments of Baron von Reichenbach and Dr. W. J. Kilner on the human aura.

He sought constantly an expression of the essential principle behind the whole of life, that vast bewildering mystery which the nineteenth century novelist Charles Kingsley once described in a letter:

When I walk the fields I am oppressed every now and then with an innate feeling that everything I see has a meaning, if I could but understand it. And this feeling of being surrounded with truths which I cannot grasp, amounts to an indescribable awe sometimes! Everything seems to be full of God's reflex, if we could but see it. Oh! how I have prayed to have the mystery unfolded, at least hereafter. To see, if but for a moment, the whole harmony of the great system! To hear once the music which the whole universe makes as it performs His bidding!

In *The Great Secret*, Maeterlinck comes within a hairsbreadth of the secret itself.

He was nearly sixty years of age when he wrote this summing-up of his life quest for wisdom. Thirty-two years earlier, as a young man, his mystical sense had been awakened by the writing of Plotinus, Jacob Boehme, the poet Novalis, and the books of Ruysbroeck, the great Flemish mystic, whose *Adornment of the Spiritual Marriage* Maeterlinck translated into French in 1889. Then he studied those shining words of an ecstatic inner vision of spiritual love which he momentarily shared:

And the loving soul cannot give itself wholly to God, nor perfectly receive God, for all that it receives is but a little thing as compared with that which it lacks, and counts as nothing in its eager emotion. And so it is disturbed, and falls into impatience, and into the strong passion of love; for it can neither do without God nor have Him, reach His depth nor His height, follow nor forsake Him. And this is the storm and the spiritual plague of which I have spoken; for no tongue can describe the many storms and agitations which arise from the two sides of love . . .

Later in life Maeterlinck was obliged to forego this luminous passion in working out the everyday duties and desires of his own destiny. He fell in love, experiencing all the joys and sorrows of physical and emotional life, and if he still brooded over death and destiny he also tasted the pleasures of the connoisseur, the fame and fortune of being a great literary figure. As a lover and husband, as an internationally successful author, Maeterlinck grounded his mystical awareness in the emotions and sensory ties of worldly life which are the inescapable consequence of incarnation for individual souls and bodies.

Perhaps he was sometimes snared by the everyday world, by his fondness for good food and wine and a dignified establishment, yet he never lost his insight nor did he betray his inner vision. The mystic experience, once known, may become remote in the day to day preoccupations of the material life but it can never be entirely forgotten.

It seems that in his later life Maeterlinck came to know truth chiefly through his intellect, thus becoming what Eastern religion would call a "Jnani"—one who has practised the *yoga* of knowledge.

It was in the Vedic revelation of the ancient Hindu sages that Maeterlinck found the purest and most majestic statements of the Great Secret, of that mystery from which we all come and to which we return. Do not be misled by Maeterlinck's nominal case for an invincible agnosticism, nor his paradoxical conclusion that the Great Secret is that all things are secret. These are not statements to be taken literally at face value, since the real truth is that the Great Secret cannot be known by *concepts*, by words and books, but only by direct transcendental awareness. Maeterlinck knew this very well from his early study of Ruysbroeck.

It is also a fundamental tenet of the ancient wisdom of India, which Maeterlinck knew instinctively held the most secret keys, that truth cannot be known simply by hearing it expounded or by studying sacred texts and commentaries. There must be a creative change in the individual, a purification of the faculties so that the supreme wisdom of the Vedas and Upanishads become self-evident *as a fact of experience*—not a didactic statement. The whole system of *Yoga* is concerned with such purification at all levels, involving certain austerities and the practice of a splendid moral code. Many of these morals have been the essential basis of most religions and also the social contract between individuals and society, although seldom practised with full integrity.

In the important spiritual exercise of meditation, the ancient sages distinguished many different levels of consciousness far beyond the concepts of philosophical discussion. Intellectual understanding of great refinement was only essential in order to develop discrimination—afterwards the intellect and the individual ego were transcended in the mystical trance of *samadhi*.

We cannot assert that Maeterlinck's investigation of the Great Secret would have been any the wiser had he followed the full *yoga* disciplines of austerity and renunciation. Although the Indian sages stressed the necessity for these things in order to enhance metaphysical understanding, these were the exercises of spiritual athletes who had reached the final stages of their lives, had tasted and exhausted worldly pleasure and pains, had performed their duties, and now wished to know only the Great Secret before passing into the unknown.

That inspiring Hindu scripture the *Bhagavata Gita* explains that true renunciation is not simply the giving up of possessions and relationships but the renunciation of *attachment* to these things. The true "Jnani" or enlightened soul need not become a wandering *sadhu* but can live in this world and play his part surrounded by all that life has to offer—yet with the poised dispassion of the skilful actor on a stage, giving a fine performance with true feeling but never for one moment losing the secret of a deeper identity and mystical purpose. For such a renunciate the secret is not unknowable —it is *incommunicable*, a cosmic awareness that must culminate in a total affirmative silence.

It is more accurate, then, to accept Maeterlinck's apparent pessimistic agnosticism as an expression of humility in the face of the vastness of the Great Secret, like those wonderful lines of the naturalist Fabre that Maeterlinck himself quoted in his own essay on "The Insect World":

> Because I have stirred a few grains of sand on the shore, am I in a position to know the depths of the ocean? Life has unfathomable secrets. Human knowledge will be erased from the archives of the world before we possess the last word that a gnat has to say to us . . .

You will not find these infinite truths in any one book except obliquely, in implications, but this present work points in the right direction. It is easy to cavil at details on which there might be valid scholarly dissent—such things are the marginalia of all inspired works. There are gaps, too, which other writers may one day fill in, particularly the difficult question of the evolution of consciousness in the prehistory of man. Although scientists recognize a human ancestry more than 600,000 years before the Christian era, there is no reliable archaeological evidence for or against those vaster cycles of creation and dissolution stated by the sages of ancient India. Some of these questions may be forever beyond formal evidence.

In his fine work *Our Eternity* which dealt with the tremendous fact of death that gives meaning to life, Maeterlinck had written:

> But do not expect that anyone on this earth will utter the word that will put an end to our uncertainty . . . If there were no more insoluble questions or impenetrable problems, the infinite would not be infinite; and then it would be necessary for all time to curse the fate that had placed us in a universe suited to our intelligence. All that exists would be no more than a prison from which there was no escape . . .

The real prison is, of course, the limited body, senses and mind of individual souls in the world of time, space and causality. It is not so much that the individual soul should expect to possess an infinite secret—no man can hope to put the universe in his pocket—but rather that the secret itself should some time overwhelm the separateness of the individual soul. Until that ecstatic timeless moment there is always a mystery which humbles our ignorance and deepens our sense of wonder.

Meanwhile Maeterlinck's book is a valuable meditation, a master-key to that secret doctrine that runs through the whole tangled story of metaphysical, occult, psychical and mystical knowledge. It is a wise and stimulating guide to the most important question that has exercized mankind over thousands of years and which every individual must face sooner or later.

It is peculiarly appropriate that in his own language the name of Maeterlinck means "The Measurer."

London, England   LESLIE SHEPARD
1969

CONTENTS

THE GREAT SECRET

CHAPTER I

PROLOGUE

I

DO not look to find in this volume a history
of occultism, or a methodical monograph
on the subject. To such a work one would
need to devote whole volumes, which would of
necessity be filled with a great measure of that
very rubbish which I wish above all to spare the
reader. I have no other aim than to tell as
simply as possible what I have learned in the
course of some years that were spent in these
rather discredited and unfrequented regions.

I bring thence the impressions of a candid
traveler who has traversed them rather as one
seeking to observe than as a believer. These
pages contain, if you will, a kind of summary, a
provisional stock-taking. I know nothing that
may not be learned by the first comer who will
travel the same road. I am not an initiate;
I have sat at the feet of no mysterious and evan-
escent masters, coming from the ends of the

earth, or from another world, expressly to reveal to me the ultimate verities and to forbid me to repeat them. I have had no access to those secret libraries, to those hidden sources of the supreme wisdom which, it seems, are somewhere to be found but will always be for us as though they were not, since those who win through to them are condemned, on pain of death, to an inviolable silence. Neither have I deciphered any incomprehensible books of magic, nor found a new key to the sacred books of the great religions. I have but read and studied most of what has been written of these matters, and amidst an enormous mass of documents, absurd, puerile, tedious, and useless, I have given my attention to those works of outstanding value which are really able to teach us something that we do not find elsewhere. In thus clearing the approaches to an inquiry that is only too often encumbered by a wearisome amount of rubbish, I shall perhaps facilitate the task of those who may wish, and be able, to go farther than I have traveled.

2

Thanks to the labors of a science which is comparatively recent, and more especially to the researches of the students of Hindu and Egyptian antiquities, it is very much easier today than it was not so long ago to discover the source, to ascend the course and unravel the underground network of that great mysterious river which since the beginning of history has been flowing beneath all the religions, all the faiths, and all the philosophies: in a word, beneath all the visible and every-day manifestations of human thought. It is now hardly to be contested that this source is to be found in ancient India. Thence in all probability the sacred teaching spread into Egypt, found its way to ancient Persia and Chaldea, permeated the Hebrew race, and crept into Greece and the north of Europe, finally reaching China and even America, where the Aztec civilization was merely a more or less distorted reproduction of the Egyptian civilization.

There are thus three great derivatives of primitive occultism, Arya-Hindu or Atlanto-Hindu: (1) the occultism of antiquity—that is, the Egyptian, Persian, Chaldean, and Hebrew occultism and that of the Greek mysteries; (2) the Hebrew-Christian esoterism of the Essenes, the Gnostics, the Neoplatonists of Alexandria, and the cabalists of the middle ages; and (3) the modern occultism, which is more or less permeated by the foregoing, but which, under the somewhat inaccurate label of occultism, denotes more especially, in the language of the theosophists, the spiritualism and metapsychism of to-day.

3

As for the sources of the primary source, it is almost impossible to rediscover them. Here we have only the assertions of the occultist tradition, which seem, here and there, to be confirmed by historical discoveries. This tradition attributes the vast reservoir of wisdom that somewhere took shape simultaneously with the origin of man, or even if we are to credit it, before his advent upon this earth, to more spiritual entities, to beings less entangled in matter, to psychic organisms, of whom the last-comers, the Atlantides, could have been but the degenerate representatives.

From the historical point of view we have absolutely no documents whatever if we go back a greater distance than five, or six, or perhaps seven thousand years. We cannot tell how the religion of the Hindus and Egyptians came into being. When we become aware of it we find it already complete in its broad outlines, its main principles. Not only is it complete, but the farther back we go the more perfect it is, the more unadulterated, the more closely related to the loftiest speculations of our modern agnosticism. It presupposes a previous civilization, whose duration, in view of the slowness of all human evolution, it is quite impossible to estimate. The length of this period might in all probability be numbered by millions of years. It is here that the occultist tradition comes to our aid. Why should this tradition, a priori, be despised and rejected, when almost all that we know of these primitive religions is likewise founded on oral tradition—for the written texts are of much later date,—and when, moreover, all that this tradition teaches us displays a singular agreement with what we have learned elsewhere?

4

At all events, even if we have need of occult tradition to explain the origin of this wisdom, which to us, with good reason, has a savor of the superhuman, we can very well dispense with it in all that concerns the essential nature of this same wisdom. It is contained, in all its integrity, in authentic texts, to which we can assign a place in history; and in this connection the modern theosophists, who profess to have had at their disposal certain secret documents, and to have profited by the extraordinary revelations with which the adepts or Mahatmas, members of a mysterious brotherhood, are supposed to have favored them, have taught us nothing that may not be read in the writings accessible to any Orientalist. The factors which distinguish the occultists—for example, the theosophists of Blavatski's school, which

7

dominates all the rest—from the scientific Indianists and Egyptologists are in nowise connected with the origin, the plan, and the purpose of the universe, the destiny of the earth and of man, the nature of divinity, and the great problems of ethics; they are, almost exclusively, problems touching the prehistoric ages, the nomenclature of the emanations of the unknowable, and the methods of subduing and utilizing the unknown energies of nature.

Let us first of all consider the points upon which they are agreed; which are, for that matter, the most interesting, for all that deals with the prehistoric era is of necessity hypothetical and the names and functions of the intermediary gods possess only a secondary interest; while as for the utilization of unknown forces, this is rather the concern of the metapsychical sciences to which we shall refer in a later chapter.

5

"What we read in the 'Vedas,' " says Rudolph Steiner, one of the most scholarly and, at the same time, one of the most baffling of contemporary occultists; "What we read in the 'Vedas,' those archives of Hindu wisdom, gives us only a faint idea of the sublime doctrines of the ancient teachers, and even so these are

Prologue

not in their original form. Only the gaze of the clairvoyant, directed upon the mysteries of the past, may reveal the unuttered wisdom which lies hidden behind these writings."

Historically it is highly probable that Steiner is right. As a matter of fact, as I have already stated, the more ancient the texts, the purer, the more awe-inspiring are the doctrines which they reveal; and it is possible that they themselves are, in Steiner's words, merely an enfeebled echo of sublimer doctrines. But if we are not gifted with the vision of a seer we must be content with what we have before our eyes.

The texts which we possess are the sacred books of India, which corroborate those of Egypt and of Persia. The influence which they have exerted upon human thought, if not in their present form, at least by means of the oral tradition which they have merely placed on record, goes back to the beginnings of history, has extended itself in all directions, and has never ceased to make itself felt, but as regards the Western world their discovery and methodical study are comparatively recent. "Fifty years ago," wrote Max Müller in 1875, "there was not a scholar in existence who could translate a line of the 'Veda,' the 'Zend-Avesta,' or the Buddhist 'Tripitaka,' to say nothing of other dialects or languages."

If the historical data were to assume from the outset in the annals of mankind the significance which they were afterward to acquire, the discovery of these sacred books would probably have turned all Europe upside down; for it was, without a doubt, the most important event which had occurred since the advent of Christianity. But a moral or spiritual event very rarely propagates itself quickly through the masses. It is opposed by too many forces which would gain by its suppression. This particular event remained confined to a small circle of scholars and philologists, and affected the meta-physician and the moral philosopher even less than might have been expected. It is still awaiting the hour of its full expansion.

6

The first question to present itself is that of the date of these texts. It is very difficult to answer this question exactly; for while it is comparatively easy to determine the period when these books were written it is impossible to estimate the time during which they existed only in the memory of man. According to Max Müller there is hardly a Sanskrit manuscript in existence that dates farther back than 1000 A. D., and everything seems to show that writing was unknown in India until the beginning of the Buddhist era (the fifth cen-

Prologue

tury B. C.) ; that is until the close of the period of the ancient Vedic literature.

The "Rig-Veda," which contains 1028 hymns of an average length of ten lines, or a total of 153,826 words, was therefore preserved by the effort of the memory alone. Even to-day the Brahmans all know the "Rig-Veda" by heart, as did their ancestors three thousand years ago. We must attribute the spontaneous development of Vedic thought, as we find it in the "Rig-Veda," to a period earlier than the tenth century B. C. Three centuries before the Christian era—once more, according to Max Müller —Sanskrit had already ceased to be spoken by the people. This is proved by an inscription whose language is to Sanskrit what Italian is to Latin.

But according to other Orientalists the age of the "Chandas" probably goes back to a period two or three thousand years before Christ. This takes us back five thousand years: a very modest and prudent claim. "One thing is certain," says Max Müller, "namely, that there is nothing more ancient, nothing more primitive, than the hymns of the 'Rig-Veda,' whether in India or the whole Aryan world. Being Aryan in language and thought, the 'Rig-Veda' is the most ancient of our sacred books." [1]

Since the works of the great Orientalist were

[1] Max Müller, "Origin and Development of Religion."

11

The Great Secret

written other scholars have set back the date of the earliest manuscripts, and above all of the earliest traditions, to a remarkable extent; but even so these dates fall short by a stupendous amount of the Brahman calculations, which refer the origin of their earliest books to thousands of centuries before our era. "It is actually more than five thousand years," says Swami Dayananda Saraswati, "since the 'Vedas' have ceased to be a subject of investigation"; and according to the computations of the Orientalist Halled, the "Shastras," in the chronology of the Brahmans, must be no less than seven million years old.

Without taking sides in these disputes the only point which it is important to establish is the fact that these books, or rather the traditions which they have recorded and rendered permanent, are evidently anterior—with the possible exceptions of Egypt, China, and Chaldea—to anything known of human history.

7

This literature comprises, in the first place, the four "Vedas": the "Rig-Veda," the "Sama-Veda," the "Yadjour-Veda," and the "Atharva-Veda," completed by the commentaries, or "Brahmanas," and the philosophical treatises known as "Aranyakas" and "Upanishads," to which we must add the "Shastras," of which

12

the best known is the "Manava-Dharma-Shastra," or "Laws of Manu"—which, according to William Jones, Chézy, and Loiseleur-Deslongchamps, date back to the thirteenth century before Christ—and the first "Puranas."

Of these texts the "Rig-Veda" is incontestably the most ancient. The rest are spread over a period of many hundreds, perhaps even of many thousands, of years; but all, excepting the latest "Puranas," belong to the pre-Christian era, a fact which we must always keep in view; not because of any feeling of hostility toward the great religion of the West, but in order to give the latter its proper place in the history and evolution of human thought.

The "Rig-Veda" is still polytheist rather than pantheist, and it is only here and there that the peaks of the doctrine emerge from it, as, for example, in the stanzas which we shall presently quote. Its divinities represent only those amplifical physical forces which the "Sama-Veda," and above all the "Brahmanas" subsequently reduce to metaphysical conceptions, and to unity.

The "Sama-Veda" asserts the unknowable and the "Yadjur-Veda" pantheism. As for the "Atharva," according to some the oldest, and according to others the most recent, it consists above all of ritual.

These ideas were developed by the commen-

taries of the "Brahmanas," which were produced more especially between the twelfth and
seventh centuries before Christ; but they may
probably be referred to traditions of much
greater antiquity, which our modern theosophists claim to have rediscovered, though without supporting their assertions by sufficient
proof.

Consequently, when we speak of the religion
of India we must consider it in its entirety, from
the primitive Vedism by way of Brahmanism
and Krishnaism, to Buddhism, calling a halt,
should the student so prefer, some two or three
centuries before our Christian era, in order to
avoid all suspicion of Judo-Christian infiltration.

All this literature—to which may be added,
among many others, the semi-profane texts of
the "Ramayana" and the "Mahabarata," in the
midst of which blossoms the "Bhagavata-Gita,"
or "Song of the Blessed," that magnificent
flower of Hindu mysticism—is still very imperfectly known, and we possess of it only so much
as the Brahmans have chosen to give us.

This literature confronts us with a host of
problems of extreme complexity, of which very
few have as yet been solved. It may be added
that the translation of the Sanskrit texts, and
especially of the more ancient, are still very
unreliable. According to Roth, the true pio-

Prologue

neer of Vedic exegesis, "the translator who
will render the 'Veda' intelligible and readable,
mutatis mutandis, as Homer has been since the
labors of Voss, has yet to appear, and we can
hardly anticipate his advent before the coming
century."

In order to form some idea of the uncertain
character of these translations, it is enough to
turn, for an example, to the end of the third
volume of the *Religion Védique* of Bergaigne,
the great French Orientalist.   Here we shall
find the disputes which arose between the most
famous Indianists, such as Grassmann Ludwig,
Roth and Bergaigne himself, as to the interpretation of almost all the essential words of
the "Hymn to the Dawn" (I, 123).   As Bergaigne says, "It exposes the poverty of the
present interpretation of the 'Rig-Veda.'" [1]

The neotheosophists have endeavored to
solve certain of the problems propounded by
Hindu antiquity; but their works, though highly
interesting as regards their doctrine, are extremely weak from a critical point of view; and
it is impossible to follow them on paths where
we meet with nothing but hypotheses incapable
of proof.   The truth is that in dealing with
India we must abandon all hope of chronological accuracy.   Contenting ourselves with a

[1] *La Religion Védique d'après les Hymnes du Rig-Véda,* A.
Bergaigne; Vol. III. p. 283 *et seq.*

minimum of certainty, which undoubtedly falls
far short of reality, and leaving behind us a
possibly stupendous waste of nebulous centuries,
we will refer only to the three or four thousand
years that saw the birth and growth of the
"Brahmanas"; when we find that there existed
at that period among the foot-hills of the Himalayas, a great religion, pantheist and agnostic,
which later became esoteric; and this, for the
moment, is all that concerns us.

8

And what of Egypt? some will say. What
of her monuments and her hieroglyphics? Are
they not much more ancient? Let us listen in
this connection to the learned Egyptologist Le
Page Renouf, [1] one of the great authorities on
this subject. He holds that the Egyptian monuments and their inscriptions cannot serve as
a basis for establishing definite dates; that the
calculations based on the heliacal rising of the
stars are not convincing, as in the texts it is
probable that the transit of the stars is referred
to rather than their rising. He is, however,
convinced that according to the most moderate
calculations the Egyptian monarchy was already in existence more than two thousand
years before the Book of Exodus was written.

[1] "Lectures on the Origin and Growth of Religion as
Illustrated by the Religion of Ancient Egypt," by P. Le Page
Renouf.

Prologue

Now Exodus probably dates from the year 1310
B. C., and the date of the Great Pyramid cannot be fixed at less than 3000 or 4000 years be
fore our era. These calculations, like those
which make the Chinese era begin 2697 years
before Christ, lead us back strangely enough,
to the period assigned by the students of Indian
history to the development of the Vedic ideal;
a development which presupposes a period of
gestation and formation infinitely more remote.
For the rest, they do not deny that the Egyptian civilization, like the Hindu civilization,
may be very much more ancient. Another
great Egyptologist, Leonard Horner, between
the years 1851 and 1854, had ninety-five shafts
sunk in various parts of the Nile Valley. It
is established that the Nile increases the depth
of its alluvial bed by five inches in a century—
a depth which owing to compression should be
less for the lower strata. Human and animal
figures carved in granite, mosaics, and vases,
were found at depths of seventy-five feet or
less, and fragments of brick and pottery at
greater depths. This takes us back some
17,000 or 18,000 years. At a depth of thirty-
three feet six inches a tablet was unearthed,
bearing inscriptions which a simple calculation
shows to have been nearly 8000 years old.
The theory that the excavators may have hit,
by chance, upon wells or cisterns must be aban-

doned, for the same state of affairs was proved
to exist everywhere. These proofs, it may be
remarked, furnish yet one more argument in
support of the occultist traditions as regards the
antiquity of human civilization. This prodigious antiquity is also confirmed by the astronomical observations of the ancients. There is,
for example, a catalogue of stars known as the
catalogue of Súrya-Siddhânta; and the differ-
ences in the position of eight of these fixed
stars, taken at random, show that the Súrya-
Siddhânta were made more than 58,000 years
ago.

9

Was Egypt or India the direct legatee of
the legendary wisdom bequeathed by more
ancient peoples, and notably by the probable
Atlantides? In the present state of our knowledge, without relying upon occultist traditions,
it is not yet possible to reply.

Less than a century ago virtually nothing
was known of ancient Egypt. The little that
was known was based upon hearsay and the
more or less fantastic legends collected by later
historians, and above all on the divagations of
the philosophers and theurgists of the Alexandrian period. It was only in 1820 that Jean-
François Champollion, thanks to the threefold
text of the famous Rosetta Stone, found the

Prologue

key to the mysterious writing that covers all the monuments, all the tombs, and almost every object of the land of the Pharaohs. But the working out of the discovery was a long and difficult business, and it was almost forty years later that one of Champollion's most illustrious successors, de Rougé, was able to say that there was no longer any Egyptian text that could not be translated. Innumerable documents were deciphered and as regards the material sense of most of the inscriptions an all but absolute certainty was attained.

Nevertheless it seems more and more probable that beneath the literal meaning of the religious inscriptions another and an impenetrable meaning is concealed. This is the hypothesis toward which the most objective and most scientific Egyptologists have inevitably tended, in view of the antiquity of many of the words employed, although they immediately add that it cannot be definitely confirmed. It is therefore highly probable that beneath the official religion taught to the vulgar, there was another reserved for the priests and the initiate, and here the theory which the scholars are compelled to entertain once more confirms the assertions of the occultists, and notably those of the Neoplatonists of Alexandria, as regards the Egyptian mysteries.

10

However this may be, there are texts as to whose authenticity there is not the slightest doubt—the "Book of the Dead," the "Books of Hymns," and Ptahhoteph's "Collection of Moral Sentences"—the most ancient book in the world, since it is contemporary with the pyramids—and many more, which enable us to form a very exact idea of the (at first) lofty morality, and above all of the fundamental theosophy of Egypt, before this theosophy was corrupted to satisfy the common people and transformed into a monstrous polytheism, which, for that matter, was always more apparent than real.

Now the older these texts the more closely does their teaching approximate to the Hindu tradition. Whether they are in fact earlier or later than the latter is after all a question of secondary importance; what interests us more deeply is the problem of their common origin, a sole and immemorial origin whose probability increases with every step adventured into the prehistoric ages.

The farther back we go the more plainly is this agreement upon the essential points revealed. For example the ideal which the Egyptian religion, in its beginnings, conceived of God. We shall find a little farther on the

Prologue

Hindu original or replica, just as we shall have occasion to compare the two theogonies, the two cosmogonies, the two systems of ethics, which are evidently the sources of all the theogonies, all the cosmogonies, and all the ethical systems of humanity.

For the Egyptian who has preserved the faith of the earliest days there is only one sole God. "There is none other God than He." "He is the sole living Being in substance and in truth." "Thou art alone and millions of living beings proceed from Thee." "He hath created all things, and He alone is uncreated." "In all times and places, He is the sole substance and is unapproachable." "He is One, the only One." "He is yesterday, to-day, and to-morrow." "He is God by God created, existing of Himself—the twofold Being, self-begotten, the Begetter of all since the beginning."

"It is more than five thousand years,"—says de Rougé, "since men first sang in the valley of the Nile the hymn to the unity of God and the immortality of the soul. . . . In this belief in the unity of the Supreme God and His attributes as Creator of and Lawgiver to Man, whom he endowed with an immortal soul, we have the primitive conceptions, encrusted like indestructible diamonds in the mythological

21

superfetations accumulated by the centuries which have passed over this ancient civilization." [1]

It is true that we have not here, in this definition of the Deity, the penetration and subtlety, the metaphysical spaciousness, the happiness of expression, the verbal magnificence—in a word, the genius,—which we shall find in the Hindu definitions. The Egyptian temperament is colder, drier, more sober, less graceful, more realistic; it has a more concrete imagination, which is not fired by the inaccessible, the infinite, as is the spirit of the Asiatic peoples. Moreover, we must not lose sight of the fact that we are not yet acquainted with the secret meaning which may lie hidden beneath these definitions. But at all events, as we understand them, the idea expressed is the same, denoting a single origin which, in conformity with esoteric tradition and pending further enlightenment, we may call the Atlantean idea. This supposition, incidentally, is confirmed by the famous passage in Timæus, according to which, as is stated by the Egyptian priest speaking to Solon, Egypt twelve thousand years ago, had an Atlantean colony.

[1] De Rougé, *Annales de la Philosophie Chrétienne;* Vol. XX, p. 327.

Prologue

As for Mazdeism or Zoroastrianism, the third of the great religions, the problem of its derivation is a simpler one, although that of its chronology is equally complicated. Zoroaster, or rather one of the Zoroasters—the last of them,—lived, according to Aristotle, in the seventh century before Christ. Pliny places him a thousand years before Moses, and Hermippus of Smyrna, who translated his works into Greek, four thousand years before the fall of Troy, and Eudoxius six thousand years before the death of Plato.

Modern science, as Edouard Schuré has demonstrated, deriving his proofs from the scholarly research of Eugène Burnouf, Spiegel, James Darmesteter, and Harlez, declares that it is not possible to determine the period of the great Iranian philosopher who wrote the "Zend-Avesta"; but in any case he places him 2500 years B. C. Max Müller, on the other hand, gives us proof that Zoroaster, or Zarathustra, and his disciples lived in India. "Some of the Zoroastrian gods," he says, "are only reflections, distortions, of the primitive and authentic gods of the 'Vedas.'"

Here, then, there is not the slightest doubt as to the priority of the Hindu books, and here at the same time is yet another confirmation of the fabulous antiquity of these books or traditions.

These preliminary observations, which would require volumes for their exposition, are enough—and for the moment it is this that concerns us—to prove that the teaching which we find, in the after ages, at the bottom of all the religions, in the shape of mysteries, initiations, and secret doctrines, dates, according to the most cautious calculations, from thousands of years ago. They will suffice, at all events, to dispel the somewhat puerile argument of those who maintain that it is comparatively recent and has been influenced by the Judo-Christian revelations. This argument is no longer seriously maintained, but there are those who evade the difficulty by saying: Yes, there are truths in this primitive religion, and even texts which can be more or less definitely dated, antecedent to Moses and to Christ; but who can sift from these the successive interpolations which have transformed them?

There are in India, it appears, more than twelve hundred texts of the "Vedas" and more than 350 of the "Laws of Manu," to say nothing of those of the sacred books which the Brahmans have not surrendered to us; and it cannot be denied that there are obvious interpolations in these texts and in the doctrines

Prologue

which they contain. We must never lose sight of the fact that the Oriental religion which is commonly and most improperly known as Buddhism falls into three great periods, which correspond pretty closely with the three periods into which Christianity might be divided; namely, Vedism, or the primitive religion, which the Brahmans commented upon, complicating it and corrupting it to their own advantage, until it became the Brahmanism which Siddhartha Gautama Buddha, or Sakyamuni, revolted against and reformed in the fifth century B. C.

The Indianists, thanks above all to the historical landmarks afforded them by the caste system, and the changes of language and of meter, have learned to distinguish easily enough these three currents in the suspect texts, and beneath the luxuriance and complications of the interpolations the broad outlines and essential truths which are all that matter to us are always visible.

CHAPTER II

INDIA

I

LET us first of all consider the conception of Deity which was formed by these ancestors, simultaneously with the Egyptians, or, as is much more probable, before them. Their traditions may lay claim to at least five or six thousand years, and they themselves received these traditions from peoples who to-day have disappeared, their last trace in the memory of man dating back, according to Timæus and the "Critias" of Plato, one hundred and twenty centuries.

I must apologize to the reader for the inextricable nomenclature of Oriental mythology and the multiplicity of those anthropomorphic divinities whom the priests of India, like those of Egypt and of Persia, and indeed of all times and countries, were compelled to create in order to satisfy the demands of popular idolatry. I shall also spare him the ostentation of a facile scholarship, lavish of unpronounceable names, in order at once to proceed to and consider only the essential conception of the First Cause, as we find it in the remotest sources, which, if not withheld from the common people, ceased gradually to be understood by them, until it became the Great Secret of the elect among the priests and initiates.

Let us at once give ear to the "Rig-Veda," the most authentic echo of the most immemorial traditions; let us note how it approaches the formidable problem:

"There was neither Being nor non-Being. There was neither atmosphere nor heavens above the atmosphere. What moved and whither? And in whose care? Were there waters, and the bottomless deep?

"There was then neither death nor immortality. The day was not divided from the night. Only the One breathed, in Himself, without extraneous breath, and apart from Him there was nothing.

"Then for the first time desire awoke within Him; this was the first seed of the Spirit. The sages, full of understanding, striving within their hearts, discovered in non-Being the link with Being.

"Who knoweth and who can tell where creation was born, whence it came, and whether the gods were not born afterwards? Who knoweth whence it hath come?

"Whence this creation hath come, whether it be created or uncreated, He whose eye

watches over it from the highest heaven, He
alone knoweth: and yet doth He know?" [1]

Is it possible to find, in our human annals,
words more majestic, more full of solemn an-
guish, more august in tone, more devout, more
terrible? Where could we find at the very
foundation of life, a completer and more irreducible confession of ignorance? Where,
from the depths of our agnosticism, which
thousands of years have augmented, can we
point to a wider horizon? At the very outset
it surpasses all that has been said, and goes farther than we shall ever dare to go, lest we fall
into despair, for it does not fear to ask itself
whether the Supreme Being knows what He
has done—knows whether He is or is not the
Creator, and questions whether He has become
conscious of Himself.

2

Now let us hear the "Sama-Veda," confirming
and elucidating this magnificent confession of
ignorance:

"If thou sayest, 'I have perfect knowledge of
the Supreme Being,' thou deceivest thyself, for
who shall number His attributes? If thou
sayest, 'I think I know Him; I do not think I
know Him perfectly, nor that I do not know
Him at all; but I know Him in part; for he who

[1] "Rig-Veda"; X, 129.

knows all the manifestations of the gods who proceed from Him knows the Supreme Being'; if thou sayest this, thou deceivest thyself, *for not to be wholly ignorant of Him is not to know Him.*

"He, on the contrary, who believes that he does not know Him, is he that does know Him; and he who believes that he knows Him is he that does not know Him. Those who know Him best regard Him as incomprehensible and those who know nothing at all of Him believe that they know Him perfectly."

To this fundamental agnosticism the "Yadjur Veda" brings its absolute pantheism:

"The sage fixes his eyes upon this mysterious Being in whom the universe perpetually exists, for it has no other foundation. In Him this world is contained; it is from Him that this world has issued. He is entwined and enwoven in all created things, under all the varied forms of life.

"This sole Being, to whom nothing can attain, is swifter than thought; *and the gods themselves cannot comprehend this Supreme Mover who has preceded them all.* He is remote from all things and close at hand. He fills the entire universe, yet infinitely surpasses it.

"When man has learned to behold all creatures in this Supreme Spirit, and his Supreme

Spirit in all His creatures, he can no longer despise anything whatsoever.

"Those who refuse to believe in the identity of all created things have fallen into a profound darkness; those who believe only in their individual selves have fallen into a much profounder darkness.

"He who believes in the eternal identity of created beings wins immortality.

"All creatures exist in this Supreme Spirit, and this Supreme Spirit exists in all creatures.

"All creatures appear to Him as they have been from all eternity, always resembling themselves."

3

Our ancestors did their best thoroughly to examine this tremendous confession of ignorance, to people this abysmal void, in which man could not draw breath; and sought to define this Supreme Being, whom a tradition more prehistoric than themselves had not ventured to conceive. No spectacle could be more absorbing than this struggle of our forefathers of five to ten thousand years ago with the Unknowable; and in order to convey some idea of this struggle, I shall borrow their own voices, reproducing only the almost despairing terms by which they expressed themselves in the most ancient and authentic of their sacred books, which we must read without allowing ourselves to be alarmed by that incoherence of the images employed which is, as Bergaigne remarks, the daily bread of Vedic poetry.

God, they tell us, is Being. He is all things, existing and in Himself; unknowable, and the cause without a cause of all causes. He is infinitely ancient, infinitely unknown. He is all things and in all things, the eternal soul of all created beings, whom no one can comprehend. He is the unification of all material, intellectual, and moral forms of all existing beings. He is the sole primordial germ, undisclosed by all, the unknown deep, the uncreated substance of the unknown. "No, No, is His name"; and all things waver perpetually between "All things are" and "Nothing exists." "The sea alone knows the depths of the sea; space alone knows the extent of space; God alone can know God." He contains all things, yet is unknown to all; He is non-existent because He is absolute Being—that which is nothing while it is nevertheless all things. "He who is, yet is not, the eternal cause that is non-existent; the Undiscovered and the Undiscoverable, whom no created being can understand," says Manu. He is no definite thing; He is no known or visible being, nor can we bestow upon Him the name of any object. He is the secret of all secrets; He is It, the passive and latent

element. The world is His name, His image;
but it is only His former existence, which contains all things in itself, that is actually exist-
ent. This universe is He; it comes from Him,
it returns to Him. All the worlds are one
with Him, for they exist only by His will; an
everlasting will, inborn in all created things.
This will is revealed in what we call the creation, preservation, and destruction of the universe; but there is no creation properly so-
called, for, since all things have from all time
existed in Him, creation is but an emanation
of that which is in Him. This emanation
merely renders visible to our eyes what was
not visible. Similarly there is no such thing
as destruction, this being but an inhalation of
that which has been exhaled; and this inhalation, in its turn, does no more than render invisible that which was aforetime seen; for all
things are indestructible, being merely the substance of the Supreme Being who Himself
has neither beginning nor end, whether in space
or in time.

4

To have explored thus profoundly and com-
prehensively, since what our ignorance calls
the beginning, the infinite mystery of the unknowable First Cause, must obviously presuppose a civilization, an accumulation of ideas

and meditations, an experience, a degree of contemplation and a perception of the universe, which are well calculated to amaze and humiliate us. We are now barely regaining the heights whence these ideas have come down to us—ideas in which pantheism and monotheism are confounded, forming only a single complex in the incommensurable Unknown. And who knows whether we could have recovered them without their aid? Less than a century ago we still knew nothing of these definitions in their original majesty and lucidity; but they had spread in all directions, and were floating like wreckage on the subterranean waters of all the religions, and above all on those of the official religion of Egypt, in which the Nu is as unknowable as the Hindu It, and in which, according to the occultist tradition, the supreme revelation at the close of the final initiation consisted of these terrible words, dropped casually into the ears of the adept: *"Osiris is a dark god!"* that is, a god who cannot be understood, who will never be understood. They were found, likewise, adrift in the Bible; or if not in the Vulgate, in which they become unrecognizable, at least in the versions of the Hebraizers, such as Fabre d'Olivet, who have restored its actual meaning, or believe themselves to have done so. Fitfully, too, they showed beneath the mysteries of Greece,

which were merely a pale and distorted reproduction of the Egyptian mysteries. They were
visible, too, though nearer the surface, beneath
the doctrines of the Essenes, who, according to
Pliny, had lived for thousands of centuries by
the shores of the Dead Sea: *"Per sæculorum
millia,"* which is obviously exaggerated. They
drifted through the cabala, the tradition of
the ancient Hebrew initiates, who claimed to
have preserved the oral law which God gave to
Moses on Sinai and which, passing from mouth
to mouth, were written down by the learned
rabbis of the middle ages. They might be
glimpsed behind the extraordinary doctrines
and dreams of the Gnostics, the probable heirs
of the undiscoverable Essenes; beneath the
teachings of the Neoplatonists, and those of
the early Christians; as in the darkness in which
the unhappy medieval Hermetics lost their way,
amid texts which bear the marks of an ever-
increasing mutilation and corruption, following
gleams of light that grew more and more perilous and uncertain.

5

Here, then, is a great truth; the first of
all truths, the fundamental truth, that lies at
the root of things, to which we have now returned; the unknowable nature of the causeless
cause of all causes. But of this cause, or this

God, we should never have known anything had
He remained self-absorbed, had He never mani-
fested Himself. It was necessary that He
should emerge from His inactivity, which for
us was equivalent to nothingness, since the universe seems to exist, and we ourselves believe
that we live, in Him. Freed from the creeper-
like entanglements of the theogonic and theo-
logical theories that quickly invaded it on every
hand, the First Cause, or rather the Eternal
Cause—for having no beginning it can be
neither first nor second,—has never created
anything. There was no creation, since all
has existed, within this Cause, from all eternity,
in a form invisible to our eyes, but more real
than it could be if they beheld it, since our eyes
are so fashioned as to behold illusions only.
From the point of view of this illusion, this all,
that exists always, appears or disappears in accordance with an eternal rhythm beaten out by
the sleeping and waking of the Eternal Cause.
"Thus it is," say the "Laws of Manu," "that by
an alternation of awakening and repose the immutable Being causes all this assemblage of
creatures, mobile and immobile, eternally to return to life and to die." [1] He exhales himself,
or expels his breath, and spirit descends into
matter, which is only a visible form of spirit;
and throughout the universe innumerable

[1] "Laws of Manu"; I, 57.

worlds are born, multiply and evolve. He himself inhales, indrawing his breath, and matter enters into spirit, which is but an invisible form of matter: and the worlds disappear, without perishing, to reintegrate the Eternal Cause, and emerge once more upon the awakening of Brahma—that is, thousands of millions of years later; to enter into Him again when He sleeps once more, after thousands of millions of years; and so it has been and ever shall be, through all eternity, without beginning, without cessation, and without end.

6

Here again we have a tremendous confession of ignorance; and this new confession, the oldest of all, however far back we go, is also the most profound, the most complete, and the most impressive. This explanation of the incomprehensible universe, which explains nothing, since one cannot explain the inexplicable, is more acceptable than any other that we could offer, and is perhaps the only one that we could accept without stumbling at every step over insurmountable objections and questions to which our reason gives no reply.

This second admission we find at the origin of the two mother-faiths. In Egypt, even in the superficial and exoteric Egypt which is all that we know, and without taking into account the secret meaning which probably underlies the hieroglyphs, it assumes a similar form. Here, too, there is no creation properly so called, but the externalization of a latent and everlasting spiritual principle. All beings and all things exist from all eternity in the Nu and return thither after death. The Nu is the "deep" of Genesis, a divine spirit hovers above it vaguely, bearing within it the total sum of future existences; whence its name, Tum, whose meaning is at once Nothingness and Totality. When Tum wished to create within his heart all that exists, he rose up amid what things were present in the Nu, outside the Nu, and all lifeless things: and the sun, Ra, was, and there was light. But there were not three gods—the deep, the spirit in the deep, and light without the deep. Tum, exteriorized by virtue of his creative desire, became Ra the sun-god, without ceasing to be Tum and without ceasing to be Nu. He says of himself: "I am Tum; I am that which existed alone in the abyss. I am the great God, self-created; that is, I am Nu, the father of the gods." He is the total sum of the lives of all created beings. And to express the idea that the demiurge has created all things of his own essence, the famous Leyden papyrus explains: "There was no other God before Him, nor any beside Him; when He decreed His likeness, there was no mother for

Him, who was self-named [in Egyptian naming is equivalent to creating] : no father for Him who uttered this name, saying: 'It is I who have created thee.' " [1]

In order to create, the Egyptian first *thinks* and then *utters* the world. (Here already is the "Word," the famous Logos of the Alexandrian philosophers, which we shall encounter again later on.) His supreme intelligence assumes the name of Phtah; his heart, which is the spirit that moves him, is Horus, and the Word, the instrument of creation, is Thoth. Thus we have Phtah-Horus-Thoth; the Creator Spirit-Word, the trinity in unity of Tum. Subsequently, as in the Vedic, Persian, and Chaldean religions, the supreme and unknowable Deity was gradually relegated to oblivion, and we hear only of his innumerable emanations, whose names vary from century to century and occasionally from city to city. Thus, in the "Book of the Dead," Osiris, who becomes the best-known god of Egypt, states that he is Tum.

In Mazdeism, or Zoroastrianism, which is merely an adaptation of Vedism to the Iranian temperament, the supreme Deity is not the omnipotent Creator who could fashion the world as he desired; he is subject to the inflexible laws of the unknown First Cause, which is perhaps

[1] See A. Moret, *Les Mystères Egyptiens;* pp. 110 *et seq.;* and Pierret, *Études Egyptologiques;* p. 414.

38

himself. In Chaldea, that crossroads where the religions of India, Egypt, and Persia meet, matter self-existent and still uncreated, gives birth to all things; not creating because all things have their being in it, but manifesting itself periodically, when its image is reflected in the world visible to our eyes. In the Cabala the last echo, the blurred copy of the esoteric doctrines of Chaldea and Egypt, we find the same confusion; the Eternal Spirit, increate and unknowable, not understood in its pure essence, contains in itself the principle of all that exists, manifesting itself and becoming visible to man only by its emanations.

Lastly, if we open the Bible—not its restricted, superficial, and empirical translation, but a version which goes to the heart of the inner meaning, essential and radical, of the Hebrew words such as that which Fabre d'Olivet attempted,—we find, in the first verse of Genesis: "In the first beginning which is to say before all, He, Elohim, God of Gods, the existing Being, created—which does not mean made something out of nothing, but drew from an unknown element, caused to pass from its principle to its essence, the Very Self of the heavens and the Very Self of earth."

"And the earth existed, a contingent power of being in the dominion of being, and the darkness (a compressive and indurating force) was over the face of the deep (the universal and contingent power of being) ; and the breath of the God of Gods (an expansive and dilating force) moved with generative power upon the face of the waters (universal passivity)." [1]

Is it not interesting to note that this literal translation brings us very close to India, to the idea of the unknown origin, and closer still to the Hindu creation; the passing from principle to essence, the expansion of the Being of Beings who contains all things, and of the externalization, upon his awakening, of the power that was latent within him during his sleep? Let us remember that in 1875 Max Müller wrote, "Fifty years ago there was not a single scholar who could translate a line of the 'Veda.' " We must therefore believe, despite the assertion of the great Orientalist, either that Fabre d'Olivet was capable of translating it, or that he had divined the spirit of it in the traditions of the cabala, which he could not have known save for the very incomplete and inaccurate *Kabbala Denudata* of Rosenroth; or else that the Hebrew text, if it really says what he makes it say, as everything seems to prove, reproduces the Hindu sources in a singular fashion, for his translation, the fruit of long previous labors, appeared in 1815; that is, ten

[1] Fabre d'Olivet, *La Langue Lébraique restituée;* Vol. II, pp. 25-27.

or twenty years before any one had learned to read Sanskrit and the Egyptian hieroglyphs.

7

Is it possible to-day, with all that we believe we know, or rather with all that we have at last realized that we do not know, to give a more comprehensive, more profoundly negative idea of divinity than that conveyed by these religions at the beginnings of the human race, or one that corresponds more closely with the vast and hopeless ignorance which will always characterize our discussions as to the First Cause? Do we not find ourselves now at an enormous height above the more or less anthropomorphic gods that followed the supreme Unknowable of that religion which was the misappreciated mother of all the rest? Is it not to her nameless enigma that we are returning at long last, after all our protracted wanderings; after wasting so much energy and so many centuries, after committing so many errors, so many crimes, in seeking for her where she was not, far from the aboriginal summits on which she has awaited us for so many thousands and thousands of years?

8

But this admission of ignorance had to be embellished and peopled; the fathomless gulf

had to be filled; an abstraction which surpassed
the bounds of understanding, with which mankind could never be content, had to be quickened into life. And this all religions endeavored to accomplish, beginning with that one
which first made the venture.

Once more I brush aside the brambles of the
theogonies, simple at their origin but soon inextricable, to follow the broad outlines. In
the primitive religion, as we have already seen,
the unknown Cause, at a given moment of the
infinity of time, beginning once more what it
has done from all eternity, awakes, divides itself, becomes objective, is reflected in the universal passivity, and becomes, until its approach-
ing slumber, our visible universe. Of this unknown self-existent cause which divides itself
into two parts, to render visible that which was
latent in it, are born Brahma or Nara, the
father, and Nari, the universal mother, of
whom is born in his turn Viraj, the son, the
universe. This primitive triad, assuming a
more anthropomorphic form, becomes Brahma,
the creator, Vishnu, the preserver, and Shiva,
the destroyer and regenerator. In Egypt we
have Nu, Tum, and Ra; then Phtah, Horus,
and Thoth; who then became Osiris, Isis, and
Horus.

After these first subdivisions of the unknown
Cause the primeval Pantheons are filled by the

serried hosts of gods who are merely intermittent emanations, transitory representatives, ephemeral offshoots of the First Cause; personifications, more and more human, of its manifestations, its purposes, its attributes or powers. We need not examine these here, but it is interesting to note, in passing, the profound truths which these immemorial cosmogonies and theogonies almost always discover, and which are gradually being confirmed by science. Was it, for example, mere chance that decreed that the earth should proceed from chaos, take shape and be covered with life precisely in the order which they describe? According to the "Laws of Manu" the ether engenders the atmosphere; the atmosphere, transforming itself, engenders light; the atmosphere and light, giving rise to heat, produce water; and water is the mother of all living creatures. "When this world had emerged from the darkness," says the "Bhagavata Purana," which according to the Hindus is contemporary with the "Veda," "the subtle elementary principle produced the vegetable seed which first of all gave life to the plants. From the plants life passed into the fantastic creatures which were born of the slime in the waters; then, through a series of different shapes and animals, it came to man." "They passed in succession by way of the plants, the worms, the insects, the serpents, the tortoises, cattle and the wild animals—such is the lower stage," says Manu again, who adds: "Creatures acquired the qualities of those that preceded them, so that the farther down its position in the series, the greater its qualities." [1]

Have we not here the whole of Darwinian evolution confirmed by geology and foreseen at least six thousand years ago? On the other hand, is not this the theory of the Akahsa, which we more clumsily call the ether, the sole source of all substances, to which our physical science is returning? [2] One might give an infinite number of these disquieting examples. Whence did our prehistoric ancestors, in their supposedly terrible state of ignorance and abandonment, derive those extraordinary intuitions, that knowledge and assurance which we ourselves are scarcely reconquering? And if their ideas were correct upon certain points which we are able by chance to verify, have we not reason to ask ourselves whether they

[1] "Laws of Manu"; I, 20.
[2] It is true that the recent theories of Einstein deny the existence of the ether, supposing that radiant energy—visible light, for example—is propagated independently through a space that is an *absolute* void. But apart from the fact that these theories seem still to be doubtful, it should be noted that the scientific ether, to which our modern scientists have been obliged to resort, is not precisely the Hindu Akahsa, which is much more subtle and immaterial, being a sort of spiritual element or divine energy, space uncreated, imperishable, and infinite.

44

may not have seen matters more correctly and
farther ahead than we did in respect of many
other problems, as to which they are equally
definite in their assertions but which have hitherto been beyond our verification? One thing
is certain, that to reach the stage at which they
then stood they must have had behind them
a treasury of traditions, observations, and experiences—in a word, of wisdom—of which we
find it difficult to form any conception; but in
which, while waiting for something better, we
ought to place rather more confidence than we
have done, and by which we might well benefit,
assuaging our fears and learning to understand
and reassure ourselves in respect of our future
beyond the tomb and guiding our lives.

9

We have just seen that the primitive religions, and those which derive therefrom, are in
agreement as to the eternally unknowable nature of the First Cause; and that their explanations of the transition from non-being to being,
from the passive to the active, and of the generative division which gives rise to the triad,
are almost identical.

Let us here note the strange defect of logic
which dominates and spreads its shadow over
the whole problem of religion. The mother-
religions, or rather the mother-religion, tells

us that the Cause of Causes is unknowable;
that it is impossible to define, comprehend, or
imagine it; that it is It and nothing more;
that it is non-existence while it is yet preëminently and essentially Being, eternal, infinite, oc-
cupying all time and space; indeed it *is* all time
and space, having neither shape nor desire nor
any particular attribute, since it has all. Now,
from this unconditioned Something, this absolute of the absolute, of which we cannot say
what it is, and even less what it purposes—of
this, the very source of the undefinable, and
the unknowable, religion calls forth emanations which immediately become gods, perfectly comprehended, perfectly defined, acting
very definitely in their respective spheres,
manifesting a personal power and will, pro-
mulgating laws and a whole moral code with
which man is enjoined to comply. How
can entities so completely comprehended
emerge from an entity essentially unknown?
How, if the whole is unknowable, can a
part of this whole suddenly become familiar? In this illimitable and inconceivable
Something, the only thing admissible, for it is
to this that science is leading us back, where is
the point whence the gods who have been im-
posed upon us emerge? Where is the link?
Where the affinity? Where and at what
moment was the incomprehensible miracle per-

formed of the transubstantiation of the unknowable? Where is the transition which
justifies this formidable change from unfathomable obscurity, not to the possible or the
probable merely, but to the known, described
even to its smallest details?

Does it not seem as though the mother-religion—and after it all the other faiths, which
are but its offspring, more or less disguised—
must have wilfully split itself in two, or rather
that it must have taken a stupendous and wilfully blind leap into the gulf of unreason? Is
it not possible that it has not dared to deduce
all the consequences of its tremendous admission? And would it not, for that matter, have
deduced the consequences elsewhere, and precisely in the secret doctrines whose traces we
are still vainly seeking, and whose revelation
sealed forever the lips of the great initiates?

10

This suspicion, which will recur more than
once as we probe more deeply into these religions, would explain the dread cry of occultist
tradition, of which we have we have already
spoken: *"Osiris is a dark god!"* Can it be
that the great, supreme secret is absolute agnosticism? Without speaking of the esoteric
doctrines, of which we are ignorant, have we
not an all but public avowal in the word *Maya*

—the most mysterious of Indian words, which means that all things, even the universe and the gods who create, uphold, and rule it, are but the illusion of ignorance, and that the uncreated and the unknowable alone are real?

But what religion could proclaim to its faithful: "We know nothing; we merely declare that this universe exists, or, at least appears to our eyes to exist. Does it exist of itself, is it itself a god, or is it but the effect of a remote cause? And behind this remote cause must we not suppose yet another and remoter cause, and so forth indefinitely, to the verge of madness: for if God is, who created God?

"Whether He is cause or effect matters little enough to our ignorance, which in any case remains irreducible. Its blind spots have merely been shifted. Traditions of great antiquity tell us that He is rather the manifestation of a Cause even more inconceivable than Himself. We accept this tradition, which is, perhaps, more inexplicable than the riddle itself as we perceive it, but which seems to take into account its apparently transitory or perishable elements, and to replace them by an eternal foundation, immutable and purely spiritual. Knowing absolutely nothing of this Cause we must confine ourselves to noting certain propensities, certain states of equilibrium, certain laws, which seem to be its will. Of these, for the time being, we make gods. But these gods are merely personifications, perhaps accurate, perhaps illusory, perhaps erroneous, of what we believe ourselves to have observed. It is possible that other more accurate observations will dethrone them. It is possible that a day will come when we shall perceive that the unknown Cause, in some respect a little less unknown, has had other intentions than those which we have attributed to it. We shall then change the names, the purposes, and the laws of our gods. But in the meantime those whom we offer you are born of observations and experiences so wise and so ancient that hitherto none have been able to excel them."

II

While it was impossible thus to address its faithful, who would not have understood its confession, it could safely reveal the secret to the last initiates, who had been prepared by protracted ordeals and whose intelligence was attested by a selection of inhuman severity. To certain of these, then, it admitted everything. It probably told them: "In offering mankind our gods we had no wish to deceive them. If we had confessed to them that God is unknown and incomprehensible; that we cannot say what He is or what He purposes; that He has neither shape nor substance nor dwelling-place, nei-

The Great Secret

ther beginning nor end; that He is everywhere and nowhere; that He is nothing because He is everything: they would have concluded that He does not exist at all, that neither laws nor duties have any existence, and that the universe is a vast abyss in which all should make haste to do as they please. Now even if we know nothing we know that this is not so and cannot be so. We know, in any case, that the Cause of Causes is not material, as men would understand it, for all matter appears to be perishable, and perishable it cannot be. For us this unknown Cause is actually our God, because our understanding is capable of perceiving it as having a scope which is limited only by our finite imagination. We know, with a certainty that nothing has power to shake, that this Cause, or the Cause of this Cause, and so forth indefinitely, must exist, although we are aware that we can never know it or understand it. But very few men are capable of convincing themselves of the existence of a thing which they can never hope to touch, feel, hear, know, or understand. This is why, instead of the nothingness which they would think that we were offering them were we to tell them how ignorant we are of all things, we offer them as their guide certain apparent traces of purpose which we believe ourselves to have detected in the darkness of time and space."

50

12

This confession of absolute ignorance in respect of the First Cause and the essential nature of the God of Gods will be found likewise at the root of the Egyptian religion. But it is very probable that once it was lost to sight—for humanity does not care to linger in hopelessness and ignorance—it would have been necessary to repeat it to the initiates, to state it definitely, to emphasize it and to deduce its consequences; and, thus revealed in its entirety, it may have become the foundation of the secret doctrine. We find, in fact, that the makers of the subsequent theogonies were eager to forget the confession recorded on the first pages of the sacred books. They no longer took it into account; they thrust it back into the darkness of the beginning, the night of the incomprehensible. No longer was it discussed, for men concerned themselves now only with the gods who had issued from it, forgetting always to add that having emanated from the inexpressible unknown they must necessarily, essentially and by definition, participate in its nature, and must be equally unknown and unknowable. It may therefore be the case that the secret doctrine reserved to the high priests led them to a more accurate conception of the primordial truth.

The Great Secret

There was in all probability no need to add further explanations to this confession since it destroys the very grounds of all possible explanations. What, for example, could the initiates be told on the subject of the first and most formidable of all enigmas, which is encountered immediately following that of the Cause of Causes—the origin of evil? The exoteric religions solved the riddle by dividing and multiplying their gods. This was a simple and easy procedure. There were gods of light who represented, and did, good; and there were gods of darkness who represented, and did, evil; they fought one another in all the worlds, and although the good gods were always the more powerful they were never completely victorious in this world. We shall find the most definite types of this dualism in the mythology of the "Avesta," in which they take the names of Ormuz and Ahriman; but by other names, and in other shapes, and indefinitely multiplied, we shall find them in all religions—even in Christianity, in which Ahriman becomes the prince of devils.

But what could the initiates have been told? The modern theosophists who profess to unveil at least a portion of the secret doctrines, by subdividing in a similar fashion the manifestations of the unknown origin, do no more than reproduce in another shape the too facile explanations of exoteric religion, so that they remain as far removed from the source of the enigma as the exoteric doctrine itself; and in the whole domain of occultism we do not find even a shadow of the beginning of an explanation which differs otherwise than in its terms from those of the official religions. We do not know, then, what was revealed to them; and it is likely enough that, just as in the case of the mysterious First Cause, they had to be told that no one knew anything. In all probability it was impossible to tell them anything that the optimistic philosophies of to-day could not tell us; namely, that evil does not exist of itself, but only from our point of view; that it is purely relative, that moral evil is but a blindness or a caprice of our judgment, while physical evil is due to a defective organization or an error of sensibility; that the most terrible pain is only pleasure incorrectly interpreted by our nerves, just as the keenest pleasure is already pain. This may be true; but we wretched human beings, and above all the lower animals whose only life is this one, have a right to demand a few supplementary explanations, if, as is only too often the case, this life is merely a tissue of intolerable suffering.

The initiated must have been given such explanations. They were referred to reincarnation, to theories of expiation and purification.

But these hints, valuable enough if we admit the hypothesis of intelligent gods whose intentions are known, are less defensible when we are dealing with an unknowable Cause, to which we cannot attribute intelligence or will without denying that they are unknown. If the adepts were ever given any other explanation, of a nature to impose itself upon them, this explanation should have contained the sovereign key of the enigma; it should have revealed all the mysteries. But not even the shadow of this chimerical key has come down to us.

13

Uncertain though its foundations may be, since they rest only on the unknowable, the fact remains that this primitive religion has handed down to us an incomparable body of doctrine touching the constitution and evolution of the universe, the duration of the transformations of the stars and the earth, time, space, and eternity, the relations between matter and mind, the invisible forces of nature, the probable destiny of mankind, and morality. The esoterism of all the religions, from that of Egypt perhaps, and in any case from those of Persia and Chaldea, and the Greek mysteries, down to the Hermetics of the middle ages, benefited by this doctrine, deriving from it the most important and most reliable elements of its prestige, by attributing them to a secret revelation, until the discovery of the sacred books of India made known their actual source and propounded a fresh enigma. Fundamentally esoterism was never anything more than a more learned cosmogony, a more rational, more majestic, and purer theogony, a loftier morality than that of the vulgar religions; moreover it possessed, for the preservation or defense of its doctrines, the secret, painfully transmitted and often terribly obscured, of the manipulation of certain forgotten forces. To-day we are able, beneath all its deformations, all its disguises, and all its masks, which are sometimes dreadfully distorted, to recognize the same countenance. From this point of view it is certain that since the publication and translation of the authentic texts, occultism, as it was still understood scarcely more than fifty years ago, has lost three fourths of its richest territories. Notably it has lost almost all doctrinal interest except as a means of verification, since we are now able to learn, at the very source from which it used to flow so grudgingly, all that it used secretly to teach: on the subject of God or the gods; the origin of the world; the immaterial forces which govern it; heaven and hell, as understood by the Jews, Greeks, and Christians; the constitution of the body and the soul, the destiny of the latter, its responsibilities, and its life beyond the tomb.

On the other hand, if these ancient and authentic texts having at last been translated, prove that nearly all the affirmations of occultism, from the doctrinal point of view, were not purely imaginary but were based on real and immemorial traditions, they permit us likewise to suppose that all its assertions in other respects, and especially with regard to the utilization of certain unknown energies, may be not purely chimerical; and in this way it gains on the one hand what it loses on the other. In fact, while we possess the more important of the sacred books of India, it is almost certain that there are others with which we are not yet acquainted, just as it is highly probable that we have still to fathom the hidden meaning of many of the hieroglyphs. It may therefore be a fact that the occultists became acquainted with these writings or these oral traditions by infiltrations such as those which we have remarked. It would seem that the traces of such infiltrations are perceptible in their biology, their medicine, their chemistry, their physics, their astronomy, and especially in all that touches on the existence of the more or less immaterial entities who appear to live with and around us. In this connection occultism still retains an interest and deserves an

attentive and methodical study which might ef-
fectively support and perhaps participate in
the investigations which the independent and
methodical metapsychists have on their part
undertaken in respect of the same subject.

14

As for the primitive tradition, while it has
lost the prestige attaching to occultism, and
while on the other hand its foundations are in-
admissible in that it derives all its precepts and
all its affirmations from a source which it has
itself declared to be forever inaccessible, incomprehensible, and unknowable, it is none the
less true, if we ignore this defective foundation, that these affirmations and precepts are
the most unlooked-for, the loftiest, the most
admirable and the most plausible that mankind has hitherto known.

Have we the right, for example, to reject a
priori, as a puerile fancy, wholly unsupported,
the conception of the Fall of Man, which we
cannot verify, when close beside it, almost contemporary with it, we find another disaster,
equally general; that of the world-wide, prehistoric deluges and cataclysms which the
geologists have actually verified? With what
profound truth may not this legend of a super-
humanity, happier and more intelligent than
ours, correspond? So far we know nothing of

it; but neither did we know what corresponded with the tradition of the great catastrophes before the annals of these upheavals, inscribed in the bowels of the earth, revealed to us what had occurred. I might mention a large number of traditions of this sort, the intuitions of genius or immemorial truths, to which science is to-day returning, or is at least discovering their vestiges. I have already spoken of the successive appearance of the various forms of life precisely in the order assigned to them by the paleontologists. To these we must add the preponderant part played by the ether, that cosmic, imponderable fluid, the bridge between mind and matter, the source of all that which the primitive religion called *Akahsa,* and which by constant repetition, becomes the *Telesma* of Hermes Trismegistus, the living fire of Zoroaster, the generative fire of Herodotus, the *ignis subtillissimus* of Hippocrates, the astral light of the cabala, the *pneuma* of Gallien, the quintessence or azote of the alchemists, the spirit of life of St. Thomas Aquinas, the subtle matter of Descartes, the *spiritus subtillissimus* of Newton, the *Od* of Reichenbach and Karl von Prel, "the infinite ether, mysterious and always in movement, whence all things come and whither all return," to which our scientists, in their laboratories, are at last obliged to have

58

recourse in order to account for a host of phenomena which without it would be utterly inexplicable. All that our chemists and physicists call heat, light, electricity, and magnetism was for our ancestors merely the elementary manifestations of a single substance. Thousand of years ago they recognized the presence and the all-powerful intervention of this ubiquitous agent in all the phenomena of life; just as they described, long before our astronomers, the birth and formation of the stars; just as the pretended myth of the transmutation of the metals, which they bequeathed to the alchemists of the middle ages, is likewise confirmed by the chemical and thermal evolution of the stars, "which," as Charles Nordmann remarks, "offer us a perfect example of this transmutation, since the heavier metals appear only after the lighter elements and when they have cooled sufficiently"; and lastly, since we must draw the line somewhere, just as they taught, in opposition to the scientists of a fairly recent period, that the duration of the universe, the ages of the earth, and the time which will elapse between its birth and its destruction, must be increased to millions of centuries, since a day of Brahma, which corresponds with the evolution of our world, contains 4320 millions of years.

15

Our forebears had also an unexpected tradition concerning yet another problem, more awe-inspiring and more essential, since it involves the fundamental law of our universe. Of this tradition humanity will never be able to verify more than an infinitesimal portion. They tell us that the cosmos, the visible manifestation of the unknown and invisible Cause, has never been and will never be other than an uninterrupted sequence of expansions and contractions, of evaporations and condensations, of sleeping and waking, of inspirations and expirations, of attractions and repulsions, of evolution and involution, of materialization and spiritualization, "of interiorization and exteriorization" as Dr. Jaworski observes, who has discovered an analogous principle in biology.

The unknown Cause awakens, and for thousands of millions of years suns and planets radiate energy, dispersing and scattering themselves, spreading throughout space; it sleeps again, and for thousands of millions of years the same worlds, hastening from every point of the horizon, attracting one another, concentrating, contracting, and solidifying until they form —without perishing, for nothing can perish— only one sole mass, which returns to the invisible Cause. It is precisely in one of these periods of contraction or inhalation that we are living. It is ruled by that vast, mysterious law of gravitation, of which no one can say whether it is electricity or magnetism or a spiritual force, although it is predominant over all the other laws of nature. If all bodies—so Newton tells us—had from all eternity, without beginning, mutually attracted one another in direct proportion to their mass, and inversely as the squares of their distances, all the substance of the universe ought by now to form nothing but an infinite mass, unless we presuppose an absolute and immovable equilibrium which would amount to eternal immobility. In the perpetual motion of the heavenly bodies, in which the displacement of an atom would disturb it, it does not seem possible that this equilibrium could exist. As a matter of fact, it is almost certain that it does not exist, and the Apex, that mysterious spot in the celestial sphere, not far from Vega, toward which our solar system is hurling itself with all its retinue of planets, may possibly be, as far as we are concerned, its point of rupture and one of the first phases of the great contraction, which, according to the latest calculations of the astronomers, will take place in 400,000 years' time.

But if it is fact that this terrible contraction must almost inevitably occur, the universe will one day be no more than a monstrous mass of

matter, compact, infinite, and probably forever
lifeless, outside which nothing could possibly
find place. Would this illimitable mass, consisting of the total sum of all cosmic matter, including the etheric and all but spiritual fluid
that fills the fabulous interstellar spaces, occupy
the whole of space, finally and eternally con-
gealed in death, or would it float in a void more
subtle than that of etheric space, and henceforth subject to other forces? It seems as
though the fundamental law of the universe
must result in a sort of annihilation, a blind
alley, an absurdity; while on the other hand, if
we deny this universal attraction or gravitation,
we are denying the only phenomenon which we
can establish as indisputable, and all the
heavenly bodies will be absolutely uncontrolled
by law.

16

The imagination, the intuition, the observations, or the traditions of our forefathers
passed this dead point. Behind their mythical
or mystical phraseology they pondered the universe, regarding it as an electrical phenomenon,
or rather as a vast source of subtle and incomprehensible energy, obeying the same laws as
those which control magnetic energy, in which
all is action and reaction; in which two antag-
onistic forces are always face to face. When
the poles of the magnet are reversed attraction

is followed by repulsion, and centripetal by centrifugal force; while gravitation is opposed by another law which as yet is nameless, but which redistributes matter and the worlds, in order to recommence a new day of Brahma. This is the *solve et coagula* of the alchemists.

This, obviously, is merely a hypothesis, some aspects of which cannot be maintained save by certain electrical and magnetic phenomena, and the properties of radioactive bodies, and which as a whole cannot of course be verified. But it is interesting to note once again that this hypothesis, the most majestic, the boldest, and also the most ancient, being indeed the first of all, is perhaps the only one to which science might rally without derogation. Here again have we not the right to ask ourselves whether our forefathers were not more far-sighted, more perspicacious than we, and whether we ourselves are capable of imagining so vast and so probable a cosmogony as theirs?

17

If now from these heights we return to mankind we shall discover intuitions or convictions of no less remarkable a nature. Without venturing ourselves amid the complexity of subdivisions which, after all, are of later date and would lead us too far afield, we shall confine ourselves to saying that in all the primitive doctrines, which agree in a most remarkable fashion, man is composed of three essential parts: a perishable physical body; a spiritual principle, a shadow or astral double, likewise perishable, but much more durable than the body, and an immortal principle which, after more or less protracted developments, returns to its origin, which is God.

Now we can prove that in the phenomena of hypnotism, magnetism, mediumship, and somnambulism, in all that concerns certain extraordinary faculties of the subconsciousness, which seem independent of the physical body, and also in certain manifestations from beyond the grave, which to-day can hardly be denied, our metaphsychical sciences are in a sense obliged to admit the existence of this astral double, which everywhere extends beyond the physical entity and is able to leave it, to act independently of it and at a distance, and in all probability to survive it, which seems once again, and in an extremely important connection, to justify the almost prehistoric intuitions of our Hindu and Egyptian ancestors.

18

As I have only too often repeated, we might multiply such instances; and when our science has thus confirmed one of these intuitions or traditions it would be only sensible to regard such as are still awaiting this confirmation with a little more confidence. The greater the number of instances in which it has been proved that they were not mistaken, the greater the chances that they are in the right in respect of other instances which cannot yet be verified. Very often these latter are the most important, being those which affect us most directly and profoundly. We must not as yet draw too general or too hasty conclusions; rather let us, as a result of these first confirmations, or beginnings of confirmations, accord a provisional and vigilant credit to the other hypotheses. When we have finally verified these first instances we shall not be out of the wood; but we shall be a great deal nearer the open sky than we were, which is as much as we have the right to hope or demand from any religious or philosophical system, or even from any science; to say nothing of the fact that the least advance here, at the center of all things, is of incomparably greater importance than an advance along a diameter or on the circumference; since from this hub or center spring all the spokes of that vast wheel of which science has barely examined the outer rim.

It must be admitted once for all that we cannot understand or explain anything; otherwise we should be no longer men but gods: or rather the one God. Apart from a few mathematical and material proofs whose essential drift we cannot after all perceive, all is hypothetical. We have nothing but hypotheses on which to order our lives, if we cease to count upon certainties which will probably never emerge. It is therefore of great importance that we should select our vital hypotheses carefully, accepting only the noblest, the best, and the most credible; and we shall find that these are almost invariably the most ancient. In the hierarchy of evolution we shall never know that central or supreme Being, nor His latest thought; but for all that we must do our best to learn a great deal more than we do know. That we cannot know everything is no reason for resigning ourselves to knowing nothing; and if branches of knowledge other than science, properly or improperly so called, are able to help us, to lead us farther or more rapidly, we shall do well to interrogate them, or at least not to reject them beforehand without due investigation, as has hitherto been done only too readily and only too often.

19

Among these assertions and these doctrines that cannot be verified we shall consider only those that concern us most intimately, and notably those which touch upon the conduct of our lives; on the sanctions, the responsibilities, the compensations, and the moral philosophy that proceed therefrom; on the mysteries of death, the life beyond the tomb, and the final destinies of mankind.

Hitherto almost all the doctrines which touch upon these points have been, for us Europeans, esoteric, hidden away in the scrolls of the cabala or the gnosis, the persecuted, humble, and haggard heirs of the Hindu, Egyptian, Persian, and Chaldean wisdom. But since the Sanskrit texts have been deciphered they are so no longer, at least in their essential elements; for although, as I have already stated, we are far from being acquainted with all the sacred books of India, and are perhaps even farther from having grasped the secret meaning of the hieroglyphs, nevertheless it is by no means likely that any fresh revelation or complete explanation would be of a nature seriously to unsettle what we already know.

20

No rule of conduct, no moral philosophy could be derived from the unknowable First Cause, the one unmanifested God. It is indeed impossible to know what He desires or intends, since it is impossible to know Him. To discover a purpose in the Infinite, in the universe, or in the Deity, we are compelled to cast ourselves adrift on the unprovable, and to

cross great gulfs of illogic of which we have
already spoken, evoking from this Cause, which
to manifest itself has divided itself, one god or
many, emanations from the Unknowable, who
suddenly become as familiar as though they had
issued from the hands of man. It is obvious
that the ethical basis resulting from this arbitrary procedure will always be precarious,
offering itself merely as a postulate which must
be accepted with closed eyes. But it is worthy
of note that, following upon this preliminary
operation, or concurrently with it, in all the
primitive religions, we shall find another which
is, as it were, its necessary and, in any case, its
invariable consequence: the voluntary sacrifice
of one of these emanations of the Unknowable,
Who becomes incarnate, renouncing His pre-
rogatives, in order to deify humanity by hu-
manizing God.

Egypt, India, Chaldea, China, Mexico, Peru
—all know the myth of the child-god born of
a virgin; and the first Jesuit missionary to
China discovered that the miraculous birth of
Christ had been anticipated by Fuh-Ke, who
was born 3468 years before Jesus. It has
very truly been said that if a priest of ancient
Thebes or Heliopolis were to return to earth
he would recognize, in Raphael's painting of
the Virgin and Child, the picture of Horus
in the arms of Isis. The Egyptian Isis, like

our own Immaculate Virgin, was represented
standing on a crescent moon and crowned with
stars. Devaki also is depicted for us bearing
in her arms the divine Krishna, while Istar,
in Babylon, holds the infant Tammuz on her
knees. The myth of the Incarnation, which is
also a solar myth, is thus repeated from age
to age, under different names, but it is in India,
where it almost certainly originated, that we
find it in its purest, loftiest, and most signi-
ficant form.

21

Without lingering over the doubtful incarnations of the Hermes, the Manus, and the Zoroasters, which cannot be historically verified, let
us consider, among the many incarnations of
Vishnu, the second person of the Brahman Trinity, only the two most famous: the eighth,
which is that of Krishna, and the ninth, which is
that of Buddha. The approximate date of the
earlier incarnation is given us by the "Bhagavat-Gita," which gives prominence to the
wonderful figure of Krishna. The Catholic
Indianists, fearing with all their too narrow
point of view, that the incarnation of Krishna
might endanger that of Christ, admit that the
"Bhagavata-Gita," was written before our era,
but maintain that it has since been revised. As
it is difficult to prove such revisions, they add

that if it is actually proved that the "Bhagavat-Gita" and other sacred books of an equally embarrassing character are really anterior to Christ, they are the work of the devil, who, foreseeing the incarnation of Jesus, purposed by these anticipations to lessen its effect. However this may be, the purely scientific Indianists—William Jones, Colebrooke, Thomas Strange, Wilson, Princeps, et al agree in the opinion that it dates from at least twelve or fourteen centuries before our era. It is in fact commented upon and analyzed in the *Modana-Ratna-Pradipa,* (a selection from the texts of the most ancient lawmakers), in "Vrihaspati," in "Parasara," in "Narada," and in a host of other works of indisputable authenticity. According to other Orientalists, since the truth must be told, the poems upon Krishna are no older than the "Mahabharata," which after all takes us back two centuries before Jesus Christ.

As for the incarnation of Siddartha Gautama Buddha, or Sakya-Muni, no doubt is any longer possible. Sakya-Muni was a historical personage who lived in the fifth century before Christ.

22

All this, moreover, is well enough known; it is needless to labor the point. But what can be the secret meaning of a myth so immemorial,

so unanimous, so disconcerting? The unknown
Cause of all causes, subdividing itself, descending from the heights of the inconceivable,
sacrificing itself, circumscribing itself, and becoming man that it might make itself known
to men! Would not all the possible interpretations be unreasonable did we refuse to see,
beneath this incomprehensible myth, yet another confession, this time more indirect, better
disguised, more profoundly concealed, of the
fundamental agnosticism, the sublime and invincible ignorance of the great primitive teachers? They knew that the unknowable could
give birth to nothing but the unknown. They
knew that man could never know God; and
this is why, no longer searching in a direction
in which all hope was impossible, they directly
approached humanity, as the only thing with
which they were acquainted. They said to
themselves: "It is impossible for us to know
what God is, or where He is, or what He purposes; but we do know that, being everywhere
and everything, He is necessarily in man, and
that He *is* man: it is therefore only in man and
through man that we can discover His purpose." Under the symbol of the Incarnation
they thus conceal the great truth that all the
divine laws are human; and this truth is only
the reverse of another truth, of no less magnitude; namely, that in mankind is the only god

that we can ever know. God manifests Himself in nature, but He has never spoken to us save by the voice of mankind. Do not look elsewhere; do not seek in the inaccessible infinity of space the God whom you are eager to find; it is in you yourself that He is hidden and it is in you yourself that you must find Him. He is there, within you, no less than in those in whom He appears to be incarnated in a more dazzling fashion. Every man is Krishna, every man is Buddha; there is no difference between the God incarnate in them and Him who is incarnate in you; but they found Him more easily than you have done. Imitate them and you will be their peer; and if you cannot keep up with them you can at least give ear to what they tell you, for they can but tell you what the God who is within you would tell you, if you had learned to listen to Him as they have listened.

23

There we have the foundation of the whole of the Vedic religion, and of all the esoteric religions which have sprung from it. But at its source the truth will hardly be enwrapped in symbols or transparent myths. There is nothing secret about it; often, indeed, it declares itself aloud, without reticence and without disguise. "When all the other gods are

no more than disappearing names," says Max
Müller, "there are left only the Atman, the
subjective self, and Brahma, the objective self;
and the supreme knowledge is expressed in
these words: *'Tat Twam, Hoc tu'; '*That is
You'; you, your true self, that which cannot be
taken from you when all has disappeared that
seemed for a time to be yours. When all
created things vanish like a dream your true
ego belongs to the Eternal Self: the Atman, the
personality within you, is the true Brahma:
that Brahma from whom birth and death divided you for a moment, but who receives you
again into his bosom, so soon as you return
to him." [1]

"The 'Rig-Veda,' or the 'Veda' of the hymns,
the true 'Veda,' the 'Veda' *par excellence,"*
continues Max Müller, "ends in the 'Upanishads,' or, as they were afterwards called, the
'Vedanda.' Now the dominant note of the
'Upanishads' is 'Know thyself'; that is, Know
the being who is the upholder of your ego;
learn to find Him and to know Him in the
Eternal and Supreme Being, the One Alone,
who is the upholder of the whole universe."

"This religion at its ultimate height, the
religion of the *Vanaprastha,* that is, of the old
man, the man who has paid his three debts,
whose eyes have beheld 'the son of his son'

[1] Max Müller, "The Origin of Religion."

73

and who withdraws into the forest, becomes purely mental; and finally self-examination, in the profoundest meaning of the word, that is, the recognition of the individual self as one with the Eternal Self, becomes the only occupation which is still permitted to him."

"Search for the Me hidden in your heart," says the "Mahabharata," the final echo of the great doctrine; "Brahma, the True God, is you yourself." This, let me repeat, is the foundation of Vedic thought, and it is from this thought that all the rest proceeds. To recover it we have no need of modern theosophy, which has but confirmed it by less familiar texts whose authority is less assured. It was never secret, but by its very magnitude it escaped the gaze of those who could not understand it, and little by little, as the gods multiplied and stepped down to the level of mankind, it was lost to sight. Its very nobility made it esoteric. In the heroic age of Vedism, when almost all men, having done their duty to their parents and their children, used to withdraw into the forest, there peacefully to wait for death, retiring within themselves and seeking there the hidden god with whom they were soon to be confounded, it was the thought of a whole people. But the peoples are not long faithful to the heights. To avoid losing all touch with them it was forced to descend, to conceal its features, to mingle with the crowd in a thousand disguises. Nevertheless we always discover it beneath the increasingly heavy veils with which it cloaks itself. "Man is the key to the universe," declared the fundamental axiom of the medieval alchemists, in a voice stifled beneath the litter of illegible texts and undecipherable conjuring-books, as Novalis, perhaps without realizing that he was rediscovering a truth many thousands of years old, indeed almost as old as the world, once more repeated it in a form scarcely altered, when he taught that "our first duty is the search for our transcendental ego."

Abandoned in an infinite universe in which we cannot know anything but ourselves, is not this, as a matter of fact, the only truth that has survived, the only one that is not illusory, and the only one to which we might still hope to return, after so many misadventures, so many erroneous interpretations in which we failed to recognize it?

24

God, or the First Cause, is unknowable; but being everywhere He is necessarily within us: it is therefore within ourselves that we shall succeed in discovering what it behooves us to know of Him. These are the two supporting piers of the arch sustaining the primitive religion and all those religions which spring therefrom, or, at least, the actual though secret doctrine of all those religions: that is, of all the religions known to us, apart from the fetishism of utterly barbarous peoples. It found these points of support in the beginning, or rather in what we call the beginning, which must have had behind it a past of thousands, perhaps millions, of years. We have found no others; we never shall find others, failing an impossible revelation—impossible in fact if not in principle,—for nothing that is not human or divinely human can reach us. We have returned to the point whence our forefathers set out; and the day on which humanity discovers another such point will be the most extraordinary day that will have shone upon our planet since its birth.

The incarnations of God, in primitive religious thought, are merely periodical and sporadic externalizations, dazzling manifestations, synthetic and exceptional, of the God who is in every human being. This incarnation is universal, and latent in each of us; but while the incarnation is regarded as a privilege for the man in whom it occurs, it is considered a sacrifice on the part of the god. Vishna willingly sacrifices himself when he descends to earth in the person of Krishna or Buddha. Has he likewise sacrificed himself by descending to earth in the rest of mankind? Whence comes this idea of sacrifice? It is a mysterious idea, dating assuredly from traditions of great antiquity; in any case, it does not appear to be purely rational, like the two previous conceptions. Nowhere is it explained why it is necessary that an emanation of God should descend into man, who is already a divine emanation. Here is a gap which is not bridged by the myth of the Fall, a myth which is likewise unexplained, unless the idea in question is based merely upon the declaration that every man who surpasses his fellows, whose sight is keener than theirs, and who teaches them what they cannot yet understand, is necessarily misunderstood, persecuted, a hapless sacrifice.

25

This idea, whether it can or cannot be explained, is none the less of great importance; for it seems to have steered primitive morality into one of its principal highways. Indeed, the conception of the unknowable, while it set free those courageous thinkers who adventured upon its naked peaks, was powerless to afford more than a negative doctrine. To be sure, it dispersed the little anthropomorphic and almost always maleficent gods, but in their place it left only a vast and silent void. On the other hand, pantheism, being as comprehensive as agnosticism, taught that as God was everywhere and all things were God, all things ought to be loved and respected; but it followed that evil, or at least that which man is forced to call evil, was divine, just as goodness is divine, so that it must be loved and respected equally with goodness. The idea was too stark, too illimitable, over-arching the two poles of the universe in too colossal a fashion; man did not dare to involve himself, did not dare to select a pathway.

Lastly, the search for the god hidden in each of us, which is one of the corollaries of pantheism, if it be left without guidance, could only have perilous consequences. There are within us all kinds of gods; that is, all sorts of instincts, thoughts, or passions, which may be taken for gods. Some are good and some evil, and the evil gods are often more numerous, and in any case more readily discoverable than the good. The true God, the supremest Deity and the most immaterial, reveals Himself only to a few. This God being thus revealed— who is, after all, no more than the best thoughts of the best of us,—He had to call upon Himself the attention of other men, to make Himself known to them, to impose Himself upon them; and it is perhaps for this reason that this singular myth, which fundamentally is probably no more than the recognition of a natural and human phenomenon, has little by little obtruded itself, struck root, and developed. It is indeed probable enough, like everything else connected with the evolution of mankind, that it did not suddenly spring from a single mind, but dimly took shape, slowly assuming a definite form in the course of unnumbered centuries of tentative experiments.

26

Without lingering longer over this enigma we shall confine ourselves to considering its influence on primitive morality, by directing the latter from the very outset toward other pinnacles than those to which the understanding pointed the way. In its absence the primitive morality which believed itself to be listening to a hidden God, but which in truth was only giving ear to human reason, would have been no more than a morality of the brain that might have been deflected toward a barren contemplation or a cold, rigid, austere, and implacable rationalism; for the reason alone, even when it reaches the loftiest heights and is taken for the voice of God, is not enough to guide mankind toward the summits of abnegation, goodness, and love. The example of an initial sacrifice curbed its severity, launching it in another direction and toward a goal of which it might perhaps in the end have caught a

79

glimpse, but which it would not have reached until very much later, after many grievous mistakes.

Is it upon this myth of incarnation that the dogma has grafted itself, although properly speaking there are no dogmas in the Oriental religions—the dogma of reincarnation in which are found all the sanctions and all the rewards of the primitive religion? The essential principle of man, the basis of his ego, being divine and immortal, after the disappearance of the body which has for the time being divorced it from its spiritual origin, should logically return to that origin. But, on the other hand, the invisible God having through the medium of the great incarnations introduced into morality the conception of good and evil, it did not seem admissible that the soul, which had not listened to its own voice or to that of the divine teachers, and which had become more or less soiled by its earthly life, should be able, at once and without previous purification, to return to the immaculate ocean of the Eternal Spirit. From incarnation to reincarnation there was only a step, which, without doubt, was taken all but unconsciously; from reincarnation to successive reincarnations and purifications the transition was even simpler; and from these proceeds the whole of the Hindu moral philosophy, with its Karma,

which after all is only the judicial record of
the soul, a record which is always up to date,
becoming worse or better in the course of its
palingeneses, until the attainment of Nirvana;
which is not, as it is too often described, an
annihilation or a dispersal in the bosom of the
Deity, nor yet, on the other hand, a reunion
with God, coinciding with the perfecting of
the human spirit freed of matter, an absolute
acquiescence in the law, an unalterable tranquillity in the contemplation of that which exists, a disinterested hope in that which ought
to be, and repose in the absolute, that is, in
the world of causes in which all the illusions
of the senses disappear; but a more mysterious
state which is neither perfect happiness nor
annihilation, but, properly speaking and once
again, the Unknowable. "That Perfection exists after death," says a text contemporary with
the Buddha, revealing the meaning of Nirvana,
which had then become esoteric:—"That Perfection both exists and does not exist after
death, that likewise is not true." [1]

As Oldenberg says very truly, citing this
pasage among several others in which the same
admission is made: "This is not to deny Nirvana or Perfection, or to conclude that it does
not exist at all. Here the spirit has reached
the brink of an unfathomable mystery. Use-

[1] "Sanyatta Nikâya"; Vol. II, fol. 110 and 199.

less to seek to disclose it. If one were finally to renounce a future Eternity one would speak in another fashion; it is the heart that takes refuge behind the veil of the mystery. From the mind that hesitates to admit eternal life as conceivable it seeks to wrest the hope of a life that passes all understanding." [1]

All this amounts to a repetition of the old fundamental admissions that in respect of essentials we know nothing and can know nothing, while it is also a fresh proof of the magnificent sincerity and the lofty and sovereign wisdom of the primitive religion.

Will all living beings end by attaining Nirvana? What is to happen in that case, and why is it, since all things exist from all eternity, that all have not already reached it? To these questions and others of a like nature the "Vedas" vouchsafed only a disdainful silence; but some of the Buddhist texts, and among them the following, discreetly reply to those who would know too much:

"This the Sublime One has not revealed, because it does not minister to salvation, because it is no help to the devout life, because it does not conduce to detachment from earthly things, to the annihilation of desire, to cessation, to repose, to knowledge, to illumination,

[1] Oldenberg, *Le Bouddha;* p. 285.

India

to Nirvana; for this reason the Sublime has revealed nothing relating to it."

27

Whatever the value of these hypotheses, it is indubitable that the moral system which we find proceeding from this boundless agnosticism and pantheism is the noblest, the purest, the most disinterested, the most sensitive, the most thoroughly investigated, the most fastidious, the clearest, the completest that we have as yet known and doubtless could ever hope to know.

This morality, as well as the enigma of incarnation and sacrifice of which we have just been speaking, and many other points which we have only touched upon, ought to be subjected to a special examination which does not enter into our design. It will suffice to recall the fact that it is based on the principle of successive reincarnations and of Karma.

The world, properly speaking, was not created; there is no word in Sanskrit that corresponds with the idea of creation, just as there is none that corresponds with the conception of nothingness. The universe is a momentary and doubtless illusory materialization of the unknown and spiritual Cause. Divided from the Spirit which is its proper essence, actual and eternal, matter tends to return to it through all the phases of evolution. Starting from beneath the mineral stage, passing through plant and animal, ending in man, and outstripping him, it is transformed and spiritualized until it is sufficiently pure to return to its point of origin. This purification often demands a long series of reincarnations, but it is possible to reduce their number, and even to set a term to them, by an intensive spiritualization, heroic and absolute, which at death, and sometimes even during life, leads the soul back to the bosom of Brahma.

This explanation of the inexplicable, despite the objections which suggest themselves, notably in respect of the origin and necessity of matter, or of evil, which remain obscure, is as good as any other, and has the advantage of being the earliest in date, apart from the fact that it is the most comprehensive, embracing all that can be imagined, setting out from the great spiritual principle to which, in the absence of any other of an acceptable nature, we are more and more imperiously compelled to return.

In any case, as it has proved, it has favored more than any other the birth and development of a morality to which man had never attained, and which, so far, he has never surpassed.

To give a sufficient idea of this morality

would require more space than is at my disposal, and destroy the scheme of this inquiry.

The wonderful thing about this morality, when we consider it near its source, where it still retains its purity, is that it is wholly internal, wholly spiritual. It finds its sanctions and its rewards only in our own hearts. There is no Judge awaiting the soul on its release from the body; no paradise and no hell, for hell was a later development. The soul itself, the soul alone, is its Judge, its heaven, or its hell. It encounters nothing, no one. It has no need to judge itself, for it sees itself as it is, as its thoughts and actions have made it, at the close of this life and of previous lives. It sees itself, in short, in its entirety, in the infallible mirror which death holds up to it, and realizes that it is its own happiness, its own misery. Happiness and suffering are self-created. It is alone in the infinite; there is no God above it to smile upon it or to fill it with terror; the God whom it has disappointed, displeased, or satisfied is itself. Its condemnation or its absolution depend upon that which it has become. It cannot escape from itself to go elsewhere where it might be more fortunate. It cannot breathe save in the atmosphere which it has created for itself; it is its own atmosphere, its own world, its own environment; and it must uplift and purify itself in order that this world and this environment may be purified and uplifted, expanding with it and around it.

"The soul," says Manu, "is its own witness; the soul is its own refuge; never despise your soul, the sovereign witness of mankind!

"The wicked say: 'No one sees us'; but the gods are watching them, as is the Spirit enthroned within them."

"O man! when thou sayest to thyself: 'I am alone with myself,' there dwells forever in thy heart this supreme Spirit, the attentive and silent observer of all good and all evil.

"This Spirit enthroned in thy heart is a strict judge, an inflexible avenger; he is Yama, the Judge of the Dead." [1]

28

Between birth and death, which is but a new birth, the "Laws of Manu" distinguish five stages: conception, childhood, the novitiate (or period of studying the sciences, divine and human), fatherhood, and, last of all, the stage of the anchorite preparing for death. Each of these periods has its duties, which must be accomplished before a man may look forward to withdrawal into the forest. While awaiting this hour, desired above all, "resignation," says Manu, "the act of returning good

[1] "Manu"; VIII, 84, 85, 91, 92.

for evil, temperance, honesty, purity, chastity, repression of the senses, knowledge of the sacred books, worship of truth, and abstention from anger: such are the ten virtues of which duty consists." [1]

The aim of our life on this earth is to set a limit to our reincarnations, for reincarnation is a punishment which the soul is compelled to inflict upon itself for so long as it does not feel that it is pure enough to return to God. "To attain the last phase," says Manu, "never again to be reborn upon this earth—that is the ideal. To be assured of eternal happiness—assured that the earth shall no longer behold the soul returning to cloak itself once again in its gross substance!"

This purification, this progressive dematerialization, this renunciation of all egoism, begins when life begins and is continued through all the phases of existence; but one must first of all accomplish all the duties of this active existence. "For all of you must know," say the sacred books, "that none of you shall achieve absorption into the bosom of Brahma by prayer alone; and the mysterious monosyllable will not efface your latest defilement, except you reach the threshold of the future life laden with good works; and the most meritorious of these works will be those which are based upon

[1] "Manu"; VI, 92.

The Great Secret

the motives of charity and love for one's neighbor."

"One single good action," says Manu further, "is worth more than a thousand good thoughts, and those who fulfil their obligations are superior to those who perceive them."

"Let the sage constantly observe the moral obligations (Yamas) more attentively than the religious duties (Niyamas) for he who neglects the moral duties is losing ground even if he observes his religious obligations."

29

There are in the life of man two plainly distinguished periods: the active or social phase during which he establishes his family, assures the fate of his posterity, and tills the soil with his own hands, fulfilling the humble duties of every-day life toward his relatives and those about him. For these yet ungodly days abound in the most angelic precepts of resignation, of respect for life, of patience and love.

"The ills which we inflict upon our neighbor," says Krishna, "pursue us as our shadows follow our bodies.

"Just as the earth upholds those that trample it underfoot and rend its bosom with the plow, so we should return good for evil.

"Let all men remember that self-respect and love for one's neighbor stand above all things.

India

"He who fulfils all his obligations to please God only and without thinking of future reward is sure of immortal happiness. [1]

"If a pious action proceeds from the hope of reward in this world or the next, that action is described as interested. But that which has no other motive than the knowledge and love of God is said to be disinterested." [2] (Let us reflect for a moment upon this saying, many thousands of years old: one of those sayings which we can repeat to-day without the change of a syllable, for here God, as in all the Vedic literature, is the best and eternal part of ourselves and of the universe.)

"The man whose religious actions are all interested attains the rank of the saints and the angels [Devas]. But he whose pious actions are all disinterested divests himself forever of the five elements, to acquire immortality in the Great Soul."

"Of all things that purify man purity in the acquisition of wealth is the best. He who retains his purity while becoming rich is truly pure, not he who purifies himself with earth and water."

"Learned men purify themselves by the forgiveness of trespasses, alms, and prayer. The understanding is purified by knowledge."

[1] "Manu"; II, 15.
[2] *Ibid.;* XII, 89.

The Great Secret

"The hand of a craftsman is always pure while he is working."

"Although the conduct of her husband be blameworthy, although he may abandon himself to other loves and may be without good qualities, a virtuous woman must always revere him as a god."

"He who has defiled the water by some impurity must live upon alms only for a full month."

"In order not to cause the death of any living creature, let the Sannyâsî [1] [that is, the mendicant ascetic], by night as well as by day, even at the risk of injury, walk with his gaze upon the ground." [2]

"For having on one occasion only, and without any ill intention, cut down trees bearing fruit, or bushes, or tree-creepers, or climbing plants, or crawling plants in flower, one must repeat a hundred prayers from the 'Rig-Veda.' "

"If a man idly uproots cultivated plants or plants which have sprung up spontaneously in the forest, he must follow a cow for a whole day and take no food but milk."

"By a confession made in public, by repentance, by piety, by the recitation of sacred prayers, a sinner may be acquitted of his offense,

[1] Literally, "the abandoner."—TRANS.
[2] "Manu"; XII, 90; V, 106, 107, 129, 154; XI, 255; VI, 68.

as well as by giving alms, when he finds it impossible to perform the other penance."

"In proportion as his soul regrets a bad action, so far his body is relieved of the burden of this perverse action."

"Success in all worldly affairs depends upon the laws of destiny, controlled by the actions of mortals in their previous lives, and the conduct of the individual; the decrees of destiny are a mystery; we must accordingly have recourse to means which depend upon man."

"Justice is the sole friend who accompanies man after death, since all affection is subject to the destruction suffered by the body." [1]

"If he who strikes you drops the staff which he has used, pick it up and return it to him without complaint."

"You will not abandon animals in their old age, remembering what services they have rendered you." [2]

"He who despises a woman despises his mother. The tears of women draw down the fire of heaven upon those that make them flow."

"The upright man may fall beneath the blows of the wicked, as does the sandal-tree, which, when it is felled, perfumes the ax that lays it low." [3]

[1] "Manu"; XI, 142, 144, 227, 229; VII, 205.
[2] "Sama Veda."
[3] "Pradasa."

The Great Secret

"To carry the three staves of the ascetic, to keep silence, to wear the hair in a plait, to shave the head, to clothe one's self in garments of bark or skins, to say prayers and perform ablutions, to celebrate the Agnihotra, to dwell in the forest, to allow the body to become emaciated—all this is useless if the heart is not pure."

"He who, whatever pains he may spend on himself, practises tranquillity of mind, who is calm, resigned, restrained, and chaste, and has ceased to find fault with others, that man is truly a Brahman, a Shraman [an ascetic], a Bhikshu [a mendicant friar]."

"O Bhârata, of what avail is the forest to him who has mastered himself, and of what avail is it to him who has not mastered himself? Wherever there lives a man who has mastered himself, there is the forest, there is the hermitage."

"If the wise man stay at home, whatever care he may take of himself, if all the days of his life he is always pure and full of love, he is delivered from all evil."

"It is not the hermitage that makes the virtuous man; virtue comes only with practice. Therefore let no man do unto others that which would cause pain to himself."

"The world is sustained by every action whose sole object is sacrifice; that is, the voluntary gift of self. It is in making this voluntary gift that man should perform the action, without respect of usage. The sole object of action should be to serve others. He who sees inaction in action and action in inaction is wise among men: he is attuned to the true principles, whatever action he may perform. Such a man, who has renounced all interest in the result of his action, and is always content, depending upon no one, although he may perform actions, is as one who does not perform them. All his thoughts, stamped with wisdom, and all his actions, consisting of sacrifice, are as though faded into air." [1]

30

There, taken at random, from an enormous treasury which is still partly unknown, are a few words of counsel, thousands of years old, which, long before the advent of Christianity, guided men of good will to the border of the forest. Then, as Manu says, "when the head of the family sees his skin grow wrinkled and his hair turn white, when he beholds the son of his son"; when he has no further obligations to fulfil; when no one has further need of his assistance, then, whether he be the richest merchant of the city or the poorest peasant

---

[1] "Vanaparva"; 13,445: "Parables of Buddhgosha"; "Cantiparva"; 5951: "Vanaparva; 13,550: "Laws of Yajnavalkya"; III, 65; "Bhagavata-Gita."

of the village, he may at last devote himself
to things eternal, leaving his wife, his children,
his kinsfolk, his friends, and, "taking a gazelle-
skin or a cloak of bark," may withdraw into
solitude, burying himself in the vast tropical
forest, forgetting his body and the vain ideas
born of it, and giving ear to the voice of the
God hidden in the depths of his being; the
voice "of the unseen traveler," in the words
of the "Brahman of the Hundred Paths"; "the
voice of him who, understanding, is not understood; of the thinker of whom none thinks;
of him who knows but is not known; of the
Atman, the inner guide, the imperishable, apart
from whom there is only suffering." He may
meditate on the infinity of space, the infinity
of reason, and "the non-existence of nothing";
may seize the moment of illumination which
brings with it "the deliverance which no one
can teach, which each must find for himself,
which is ineffable," and may purify his soul
in order to spare it, if that be possible, yet
another return to earth.

Having reached this stage, "let him not wish
for death; let him not wish for life. Like a
harvester who, at the fall of night, waits
quietly for his wages at his master's door, let
him wait until the moment has arrived."

"Let him meditate, with the most exclusive
application of the intellect, upon the subtle and

indivisible nature of the Supreme mind, and on its existence in the bodies of the highest and lowest of created things."

"Meditating with joy upon the Supreme Being, having need of nothing, inaccessible to any desire of the senses, without other society than his own soul and the thought of God, let him live in the constant expectation of eternal bliss."

"For the chiefest of all his obligations is to acquire knowledge of the Supreme Mind; and this is the first of all the sciences, for this alone confers immortality upon man."

"Thus the man who discovers the Supreme Mind in his own mind, and present in all living creatures, will show himself the same to all, and will thus assure himself of the happiest fate, that of being finally absorbed into the bosom of Brahma." [1]

"Having thus abandoned all pious practices and acts of austere devotion, applying his intellect solely to the contemplation of the great First Cause, exempt from all evil desires, his soul is already on the threshold of Swarga, while his mortal envelope is still flickering like the last glimmer of a dying lamp." [2]

31

Almost all the foregoing, let us remember,

[1] "Manu"; VI, 45, 65, 49; XII, 85, 125.
[2] *Ibid.;* VI, 96.

is long previous to Buddhism, dating from the origins of Brahmanism, and is directly related to the "Vedas." Let us agree that this system of ethics, of which I have been unable to give more than the slightest survey, while the first ever known to man, is also the loftiest which he has ever practised. It proceeds from a principle which we cannot contest even to-day, with all that we believe ourselves to have learned; namely, that man, with all that surrounds him, is but a sort of emanation, an ephemeral materialization, of the unknown spiritual cause to which it must needs return, and it merely deduces, with incomparable beauty, nobility, and logic, the consequences of this principle. There is no extra-terrestrial revelation, no Sinai, no thunder in the heavens, no god especially sent down upon our planet. There was no need for him to descend hither, for he was here already, in the hearts of all men, since all men are but a part of him and cannot be otherwise. They question this god, who seems to dwell in their hearts, their minds; in a word, in that immaterial principle which gives life to their bodies. He does not tell them, it is true—or perhaps he does tell them, but they cannot understand him—why, for the time being, he appears to have divorced them from himself; and we have here a postulate— the origin of evil and the necessity of suffering

—as inaccessible as the mystery of the First Cause: with this difference, that the mystery of the First Cause was inevitable, whereas the necessity of evil and suffering is incomprehensible. But once the postulate is granted, all the rest clears up and unfolds itself like a syllogism. Matter is that which divides us from God; the spirit is that which unites us to Him; the spirit therefore must prevail over matter. But the spirit is not merely the understanding; it is also the heart; it is emotion; it is all that is not material; so that in all its forms it must needs purify itself, reaching forth and uplifting itself, to triumph over matter. There never was and never could be, I believe, a more impressive spiritualization than this, nor more logical, more unassailable, more realistic, in the sense that it is founded only on realities; and never one more divinely human. Certain it is that after so many centuries, after so many acquisitions, so many experiences, we find ourselves back at the same point. Starting, like our predecessors, from the unknowable, we can come to no other conclusion, and we could not express it better. Nothing could excel the stupendous effort of their speech, unless it were a silent resignation, preferable in theory, but in practice leading only to an inert and despairing ignorance.

CHAPTER III

EGYPT

I

WE have already considered, in speaking of Nu, Tum, and Phtah, the idea which the Egyptians formed of the First Cause, and of the creation, or rather, the emanation or manifestation, of the universe. This idea— as we know it, at least, from the translation, probably incomplete, of the hieroglyphs,— though less striking in form, less profound and less metaphysical, is analogous to that of the "Vedas" and reveals a common source.

Immediately following the riddle of the First Cause they, too, inevitably encountered the insoluble problem of the origin of evil, and although they did not venture to probe into it very deeply, they achieved a solution of it which, though paler and more evasive, is at bottom almost similar to that of the Hindus. In the cult of Osiris spirit and matter are known as Light and Darkness, and Set, the antagonist of Ra, the sun-god, in the myths of Ra, Osiris, and Horus, is not a god of evil," says Le Page Renouf, "but represents a physical reality, a constant law of nature." [1]   He is a god as

[1] *Op. cit.;* p. 115.

real as his adversaries and his cult is as ancient
as theirs. Like them he has his priests, and is
the offspring of the same unknown Cause. So
little can he be divided from the Power opposed
to him that on certain monuments the heads
of Horus and Set grow upon the same body,
making but one god.

After the same confessions of ignorance,
here, as in India, the myth of incarnation proceeds to define and control an ethic which,
emerging from the unknowable, could not take
shape and could not be known except in and by
man. Osiris, Horus, and Thoth or Hermes,
who five times put on human form—or so the
occultists tell us—are but the more memorable incarnations of the god who dwells in each
of us. From these incarnations arises, with
less refulgence, less abundance, less power—
for the Egyptian genius has not the spaciousness, the exaltation, the power of abstraction
that mark the Hindu genius—an ethic of a
more lowly and earthly character, but of the
same nature as that of Manu, Krishna, and
Buddha; or rather of those who in the night
of the ages preceded Manu, Krishna, and Buddha. This ethical system is found in the "Book
of the Dead" and in sepulchral inscriptions.
Some of the papyri of the "Book of the Dead"
are more than four thousand years old, but some
of the texts from the same book, which were

found on nearly all the tombs and sarcophagi, are probably still more ancient. They are, with the cuneiform inscriptions, the most ancient writings of known date possessed by mankind.

The most venerable of moral codes, the work of Phtahotep, still imperfectly deciphered, contemporary with the pyramids, is clothed in the authority of an ancestry infinitely more remote. "Not one of the Christian virtues," says F. J. Chapas, one of the first of the great Egyptologists, "has been forgotten in the Egyptian system of ethics. Pity, charity, kindness, self-control in speech and action, chastity, the protection of the weak, benevolence toward the lowly, deference toward superiors, respect for the property of others, even to the smallest details, all are expressed in admirable language."

2

"I have not injured a child," says a funeral inscription, "I have not oppressed a widow, I have not ill-treated a herdsman. During my lifetime no one went a-begging, and when the years of famine came I tilled all the soil of the province, feeding all its inhabitants, and I so ordered matters that the widow was as though she had not lost her husband." [1]

[1] Inscriptions of Ameni, *Denkmäler;* II, 121.

Egypt

Another inscription commemorates "the father of the defenseless, the stay of those who were motherless, the terror of the evil-doer, the protector of the poor. He was the avenger of those who had been despoiled by the mighty. He was the husband of the widow and the refuge of the orphan."[1] "He was the protector of the humble, a fruitful palm for the indigent, the nourishment of the poor, the wealth of the feeble; and his wisdom was at the service of the ignorant."[2] "I was the bread of the hungry; I was water to the thirsty; I was the cloak of the naked and the refuge of the distressed. What I did for them God had done for me,"[3] say other inscriptions, always returning to the same theme of kindness, justice, and charity. "Although I was great I have always behaved as though I were humble. I have never barred the way to one who was worthier than I; I have always repeated what has been told me exactly as it was spoken. I have never approved that which was base and evil, but I have taken pleasure in speaking the truth. The sincerity and kindness in the heart of my father and mother were repaid to them by my love. I was the joy of my brethren and the friend of my companions, and I have

[1] Antuff-tablet, Louvre; C, 26.
[2] Borgmann, *Hieroglyphische Inschriften;* Plate VI, line 3; Plates VIII, IX.
[3] British Museum; 581.

entertained the passing traveler; my doors
were open to those who came from abroad, and
I gave them rest and refreshment. What my
heart dictated to me I did not hesitate to do." [1]

3

In the "Book of the Dead," when, after the
long and terrible crossing of the Tuat (which
is not the Egyptian Hades, as some have said,
but a region intermediate between death and
eternal life), the soul reached the land of
Menti, which later was known as Amenti, it
found itself confronted by Maât or Maît, the
most mysterious of the Egyptian divinities.
Maât may be symbolized by a straight line;
she represents the law, and the true or absolute
justice. Each of the high gods claims to be
her master, but she herself admits no master.
By her the gods live, she reigns alone upon the
earth, in the heavens and the world beyond
the tomb; she is at once the mother of the god
who created her, his daughter, and the god
himself. Before Osiris, seated upon the
throne of judgment, the heart of the dead
man, symbolizing his moral nature, is
placed in one of the scales of the balance;
in the other scale is an image of Maât. Forty-
two divinities, who represent the forty-two sins
which they are appointed to punish, are ranked

[1] Dumichen, *Kalenderinschriften;* XLVI.

behind the balance, whose pointer is watched by Horus while Tehutin, the god of letters, writes down the result of the weighing. All this is obviously merely an allegorical representation, a sort of pictoral interpretation, a projection upon the screen of this world of that which happens in the other world, in the depths of a soul or a conscience undergoing judgment after death.

Then, if the trial is favorable, an extraordinary thing come to pass, which reveals the secret meaning, profound and unexpected, of all this mythology: the man becomes god. He becomes Osiris himself. He stands forth as identified with him who judges him. He adds his name to that of Osiris; he is Osiris so-and-so. In short, he discovers himself to be the unknown god, the god that he was unawares. Hidden in the depths of his soul, he recognizes the Eternal, whom he had sought all his life long, and who, at length set free by his good works and his spiritual efforts, reveals himself as identical with the god to whom he had given ear, the god whom he had adored, seeking to draw closer to him by taking him for his model.

This, represented by a different imagery, is the absorption of the purified soul into the bosom of Brahma, the return to divinity of what is divine in man; and here too, beneath the dramatic allegory, the soul judges itself and recognizes itself as worthy to return to its God.

4

Rudolph Steiner, who, when he does not lose himself in visions—plausible, perhaps, but incapable of verification—of the prehistoric ages, of astral negatives, and of life on other planets, is a shrewd and accurate thinker, has thrown a remarkable light upon the meaning of this judgment and of the identification of the soul with God. "The Osiris Being," he says, "is merely the most perfect degree of the human being. It goes without saying that the Osiris who reigns as a judge over the external order of the universe is himself but a perfect man. Between the human state and the divine there is but a difference of degree. Man is in process of development; at the end of his course he becomes God. According to this conception God is an eternal becoming, not a God complete in himself.

"Such being the universal order, it is evident that he alone may enter into the life of Osiris who has already become an Osiris himself, before knocking at the gate of the eternal temple. Therefore the highest life of man consists in transforming himself into Osiris. Man becomes perfect when he lives as Osiris, when he makes the journey that Osiris has made. The myth of Osiris acquires thereby a profounder meaning. The god becomes the pattern for him who seeks to awaken the Eternal within himself." [1]

5

This deification, this Osirification of the soul of the upright man, has always astonished the Egyptologists, who have not grasped its hidden meaning and have not perceived that the soul was returning to the Vedic Nirvana of which it is merely the dramatized reproduction. But there are the authentic texts, and even from the esoteric point of view it is not possible to attribute another meaning to them. The basis of the Egyptian religion, beneath all the parasitical growths of vegetation that gradually became so enormous, is really the same as that of the Vedic religion. Starting from the same point of departure in the unknowable, it is the worship of and the search for the god in man and the return of man to the godhead. The upright man—that is, the man who all his life has striven to find the Eternal within himself, and to give ear to its voice,—when liberated from his body, does not merely become Osiris; but just as Osiris is other gods, so he

[1] Rudolph Steiner. *Le Mystère Chrétien et les Mystères antiques,* tr. J. Saurwein; p. 170.

too becomes other gods. He speaks as though he were Ra, Tum, Set, Chnemu, Horus, and so forth. "Neither men nor gods, nor the spirits of the dead, nor men past, present, and future, whosoever they may be, have any further power to harm him." He is "He who goes forward in security." His name is "He that is unknown to men." His name is "Yesterday, that sees the innumerable days passing in triumph along the ways of heaven." "He is the lord of eternity. He is the master of the royal crown and each of his limbs is a god."

6

But what happens if the sentence is not favorable, if the soul is not considered worthy of returning to the Eternal, of becoming once more the god that it was? Of this we know nothing. Of all that has been said in respect of punishments, expiations, and purifying transmigration, nothing is based on any authentic text. "We find no trace," says Le Page Renouf, "of a conception of this kind in any of the Egyptian texts hitherto discovered. The transformations after death, we are expressly informed, depend solely on the will of the deceased, or of his genius." [1] That is to say, of his soul. Does this not also expressly tell us

[1] Le Page Renouf, *op. cit.;* p. 183.

Egypt

that they depend entirely on the soul's judgment of itself, and that the soul alone knows and decides, like the Hindu soul burdened with its Karma, whether it is worthy or not to reenter divinity? In other words, that there is no heaven or hell, except within us?

But what becomes of it if it does not consider itself worthy of being a god? Does it wait, or does it undergo reincarnation? No Egyptian text enables us to solve the problem; nor is there any trace of any intermediate state between death and eternal beatitude. As to this point the funeral rites give us no hint. They seem to forecast for the dead man a life beyond the tomb, precisely resembling, on another plane, the life which he used to lead on earth. But these rites do not seem to refer to the soul properly so called, to the divine principle. The Egyptian religion, like other primitive religions, distinguishes three portions in man: first, the physical body; secondly, a perishable spiritual entity, a sort of reflection of the body which it survived, a shadow, or rather a double, which could at will confound itself with the mummy or detach itself therefrom; and, thirdly, a purely spiritual principle, the veritable and immortal soul, which, after the judgment, became a god.

The double that left the body, but not the

107

soul, which once more became Osiris, wandered wretchedly between the visible and the invisible worlds—as the discarnate souls of our spiritualists appear to do—unless the funeral rites came to its aid, leading it back to and keeping it by the body which it had deserted. The whole of this ritual sought only to prolong as far as possible the existence of this double, by supplying its needs, which resembled those of its earthly life, by keeping it beside its incorruptible mummy, and tying it down to a pleasant home.

The life of this double was believed to be very long. A tablet in the Louvre tells us, for example, that Psamtik, son of Ut'ahor, who lived in the time of the twenty-sixth dynasty, was a priest under three sovereigns of the Great Pyramid, who had been dead for more than two thousand years.

This idea of the double, as Herbert Spencer remarks, is universal. "Everywhere we find expressed or implied the belief that every man is double, and that when he dies his other self, whether it remains close at hand or goes far away, may return, and is capable of injuring his enemies or helping his friends."

This Egyptian double is no other than the Perisprite, the astral Body, of the occultists, that discarnate entity, that subconscious being, more or less independent of the body, that Unknown Guest, with whom our modern metapsychists are confronted, despite themselves, when they come to record certain hypnotic or mediumistic manifestations, certain phenomena of telepathy, of action at a distance, of materialization, of posthumous apparition, which would otherwise be all but inexplicable. Once again the ancient religions have here forestalled our science, perhaps because they saw farther into the future and with greater accuracy. I say perhaps; for if the life of the double, the astral body of the subconscious entity almost independent of the brain, can scarcely be contested when the living are concerned, it may still be disputed in respect of the dead. One thing is certain, that a number of extremely perplexing facts are accumulating in confirmation of this existence. It is only their interpretation that is still doubtful. But the ancient Egyptian hypothesis is becoming more and more plausible. It refuted beforehand, thousands of years ago, the capital objection so often made to the spiritualists, when we tell them that their disembodied spirits are merely poor, incoherent, and bewildered shades, anxious before all else to establish their identity and to cling to their former existence; miserable phantoms to whom death has revealed nothing, and who have nothing to tell us of their life beyond the tomb, a pale reflection of their previous existence. It is, after all, quite easy to explain why the disembodied spirit knows no more than it knew during its earthly life. The Egyptian double, of which it is merely the replica, was not the true soul, the immortal soul, which, if Amenti's judgment of it were favorable, returned to the god, or rather once more became divine. The sepulchral rites did not seek to concern themselves with this soul, whose fate was determined by the sentence of Maât: they sought only to render less precarious, less pitiable, and less liable to disintegration the posthumous life of this belated element, this species of spiritual husk, this nervous, magnetic or fluid phantom which was once a man and was now but a bundle of tenacious but homeless memories. By surrounding him with the objects of these memories they sought to alleviate the passage of the dead man to eternal forgetfulness. The Egyptians had undoubtedly examined more exactly than we have done the evidence for the existence of this double, which we are barely beginning to suspect; for their civilization (which was the heir, for that matter, of long-lived antecedent civilizations) was far more ancient than our own, and more inclined toward the spiritual and invisible sides of life. But they prejudged nothing, just as the spiritualistic hypothesis, if it were well propounded, would not involve any preconceived ideas of the destiny of the soul properly so called.

The double was not subjected to any form of trial. Whether a man had been good or bad, just or unjust, he had a right to the same funeral ceremonies and the same life beyond the tomb. His punishment or reward was in his own self: it was, to continue to be what he had been; to pursue the mode of life, whether noble or ignoble, narrow or liberal, intelligent or stupid, generous or selfish, which he had lived on earth.

Let us note that in our spiritualistic manifestations likewise there is no question of reward or punishment. Our disembodied spirits, even when they have been believers during life, hardly ever allude in any way to a posthumous trial, a hell, a heaven, or a purgatory; and if by exception they do refer to them we may almost certainly suspect some telepathic interpolation. They are, or, if you prefer it, they seem to be, just what they were during their lifetime: more or less logical, more or less cultivated, more or less intelligent, more or less headstrong, according as their ideas were more or less logical, or cultivated, or intelligent, or headstrong. They reap only what they have sown in the spiritual soil of this world.

The Great Secret

But they—and this is the only difference between them—have not been subjected, like
the Egyptian double, to the magic incantation
which, wrongly or rightly, for weal or woe, and
in violation of the laws of nature, bound the
double to its physical remains, and prevented
it from drifting like flotsam between a material
world in which it could live no longer and a
spiritual universe which it seemed it was forbidden to enter.

7

Thanks to this solicitude, thanks to this cult,
this foresight, was the double happy? I dare
not affirm as much. There is one terrible text
—the funeral inscription of the wife of Pasher-
enpath—which is the most heart-rending cry of
regret and distress that the dead have ever ad-
dressed to life. It is true that this inscription
is of the time of the Ptolemies; that is, of the
later Egypt corrupted by Greece, two or three
centuries before our era. It reveals the decadence and almost the death of this Egyptian
creed; and—what is more serious and more
alarming—in speaking of Amenti it seems to
confound the destiny of the double with that
of the immortal soul. Here is this inscription,
which shows us what uncertainty overtakes the
most firmly established and most positive reli-

gions, and how, when their course is run, they plunge us once more into the darkness of the Great Secret, into the chaos of the unknowable whence they emerged:

"Oh, my brother, my husband, do not cease to drink, to eat, to empty the cup of joy, to live merrily as at a festival! Let thy desires lead thee, day by day, and may care never enter thy heart so long as thou livest upon the earth. For Amenti is the country of lifeless sleep and of darkness, a place of mourning for those who dwell therein. They sleep in their effigies; they no longer wake to behold their brethren; they recognize neither their fathers nor their mothers; their hearts are indifferent to their wives and children. On the earth all men enjoy the water of life, but here thirst encompasses me. There is water for all who dwell upon the earth, but I thirst for the water which is close beside me. I know not where I am since I came hither, and I implore the running water, I implore the breeze upon the river bank, that it will assuage the soreness of my heart. For as for the God who is here, his name is Absolute Death. He summons all men, and all come to him trembling with fear. With him there is no respect for men or for gods; with him the great are as the small. One fears to pray to him for he does not give ear. None come hither to invoke him, since he shows no

favor to those who worship him, and pays no
heed to the offerings laid before him." [1]

8

And what of reincarnation? It is generally
believed that Egypt is preëminently the land of
palingenesis and metempsychosis. Nothing of
the sort: not a single Egyptian text alludes to
such matters. It is true that on becoming Osiris the soul had the power of assuming any
shape; but this is not reincarnation properly so
called, the expiatory and purifying reincarnation of the Hindus. All that we have been
able to learn in this connection is based principally on a passage of Herodotus, which observes that "the Egyptians were the first to affirm that the soul of man is immortal. Continually, from one living creature about to die
it passes into another in the act of birth, and
when it has traversed the whole terrestial,
aquatic, and aërial world, it returns once more
to introduce itself into a human body. This cir-
cular tour lasts for three thousand years. We
have here a theory which various Greeks, more
or less of our period, have appropriated to
themselves. I know their names, but I will not
place them on record." [2]

In the same way, all that touches on the fa-

[1] Sharpe, "Egyptian Inscriptions"; I, Plate 4.
[2] Herodotus; II, 123.

mous mysteries of the Egyptian initiation is of comparatively recent origin, dating from the time when Alexandria was seething with the traditions and theories of the Hindus, Chaldeans, Jews, and Neoplatonists. The Egypt of the Pharaohs has not told us what became of the soul that was not beatified. It is possible that it was obliged to return to earth in order to purify itself, and that the secret of this reincarnation was reserved for the initiates; just as it also is possible that texts more accurately interpreted, or others that are as yet unknown to us, will justify and explain the esoteric tradition. For the rest, it would not be surprising, as Sédir, one of the most learned of occultists, has remarked, if some part of the secrets which cannot be found in those inscriptions which we imagine are completely understood, were to come to us by way of Chaldea, since it was among the Magi, on the banks of the Tigris and Euphrates, that Cambyses, after the conquest of Egypt, exiled all the priests of the latter country, without exception and without return. However this may be, I repeat that the purely Egyptian texts do not, for the time being, enable us to solve the problem.

CHAPTER IV

PERSIA

PERSIA will not detain us long, for its religion is undoubtedly a reflection of Vedism, or, more probably, it reveals a common origin. Eugène Burnouf and Spiegel have indeed proved that certain parts of the "Avesta" are as old as the "Rig-Veda."

Mazdeism or Zoroastrianism would thus appear to be an adaptation to the Iranian mentality of Vedism, or of Aryan traditions (Atlantean, the theosophists would say) even older than Vedism. During the Babylonian captivity it permeated Chaldeism and exerted a profound influence on the religion of the Jewish nation. We owe to it, among other things—as they found their way into the Judo-Christian tradition,—the conception of the immortality of the soul, the judgment of the soul, the last judgment, the resurrection of the dead, purgatory, the belief in the efficacy of good works as a means of salvation, the revocability of penalties and rewards, and all our angelology.

Zoroastrianism sought to solve, more exactly than the other religions of antiquity, the problem of evil, by making evil a separate god, perpetually warring against the good god. But this dualism is more apparent than real. Ahura-Mazda or Ormazd (Ormuz), the absolute and universal Being, the Word, the omnipotent and omniscient Spirit, the Reality, precedes and dominates Agra-Mainyus or Ahriman, who is non-Reality—that is to say, he is all that is bad and deceptive, being in his darkness ignorant of everything; seeming as greatly inferior to Ormazd as the devil is to the God of the Christians; appearing, on the whole, merely as a sort of mimic, aping divinity, clumsily imitating its creations, but able to produce only vices, diseases and a few maleficent creatures who will be annihilated in the tremendous victory of good; for the end of the world, in the Zoroastrian system, is but the regeneration of creation. However, we are not told why Ormazd, the supreme god, is obliged to tolerate Ahriman, who, it is true, does not personify essential or absolute evil, but the evil necessary to good, the darkness indispensable to the manifestation of light, the reaction which follows action, the negative principle or pole which is opposed to the positive, in order to assure the life and equilibrium of the universe.

Moreover Ormazd himself, it seems, obeys necessity, or a natural law that is stronger than he; above all he obeys Time, whose decrees are Destiny, "for excepting Time," says the "Ulema," "all things are created, and Time is the Creator. Time in itself displays neither summit nor foundations; it has been always and will always be. An intelligent person will not ask, Whence comes Time? nor if there was ever a time when this power was not."[1]

It would be interesting to examine this religion from the point of view of its contributions to Christianity, which borrowed as much from it as from Brahmanism and Buddhism; perhaps even more. We ought also to consider, if only in passing, its ethical system, which is one of the loftiest, purest, and most nobly human that we know of. But this examination would exceed the scope of our inquiry. We owe to ancient Persia, for example, the wonderful conception of the conscience, a sort of divine power, existing from all eternity, independent of the material body, taking no part in the errors which it sees committed, remaining pure amid the worst aberrations, and accompanying the soul of man after his death. And the soul of the upright man, when crossing the bridge Tchinvat, or the bridge of Retribution, sees advancing to meet it a young girl of miraculous beauty. "Who art thou?" demands the astonished soul; "thou who seemest to me more beautiful and more magnificent than any

[1] J. Darmesteter, *Ormazd et Ahriman;* p. 320.

of the daughters of earth?" And his conscience replies: "I am thine own works. I am the incarnation of thy good thoughts, words, and actions: I am the incarnation of thy faith and piety."

On the other hand, if it be a sinner who is crossing the bridge of retribution, his conscience comes to meet him in a horrible shape, although in herself she does not change, but merely shows herself to man as he deserves to see her. This allegory, which might well be drawn from a collection of Christian parables, is perhaps 5000 to 6000 years old, and is merely a dramatic expression of the Hindu Karma. Here again, as in the tradition of Karma and that of the Osirification of the soul, it is the soul that is its own judge.

We owe likewise to Mazdeism the subtle and mysterious conception of the Fravashis or Ferohers which the cabala borrowed from Persia, and which Hebraic mysticism and Christianity have made into angels, and more particularly guardian angels. This conception implies the preëxistence of the soul. The Ferohers are the spiritual form of being, independent of material life and preceding it. Ormazd offers to the Ferohers of men the choice of remaining in the spiritual world or of descending to earth to be embodied in human flesh. It was probable from prototypes of this kind that Plato de-

The Great Secret

rived his theory of "ideas," supposing that everything has a double life, first in thought and secondly in reality.

Let me add that a phenomenon analogous to that which we have already found at work in India is here seen to repeat itself: what was public and obvious in Mazdeism gradually became secret and was reserved solely for those initiated into what the Greeks and the Jews (especially in their cabala) had borrowed from it.

CHAPTER V

CHALDEA

CHALDEA—that is to say, Babylonia and Assyria—is, like Persia, the land of the Magi and is commonly regarded as the classic home of occultism; but here again, as we saw in the case of Egypt, the legend is hardly in agreement with the historic reality.

It seems a priori that Chaldea should possess a peculiar interest for us; not because it is likely to teach us anything that we have not learned from India, Egypt, or Persia, to which it was tributary, but because it was probably the principal source of the cabala, which was itself the great fountainhead from which the occultism of the middle ages, as it has come down to us, was fed.

It was hoped that the discovery of the key to the cuneiform inscriptions—a discovery scarcely more than fifty years old,—and the deciphering of the inscriptions of Nineveh and Babylon, would result in valuable revelations concerning the mysteries of the Chaldean religion. But these inscriptions, which date from 2000, 3750, and in one instance (preserved in

the British Museum) 4000 years before Christ,
and whose interpretation moreover is far more
uncertain and controversial than that of the
hieroglyphs or the Sanskrit texts, have yielded
us only royal biographies, inventories of conquests, incantatory formulæ, litanies, and
psalms which served as models for the Hebrew
psalms. From these we perceive that the
basis of the very primitive religion of the Su-
mirs or Sumerians and the Accads or Acca-
dians who peopled lower Chaldea before the
Semitic conquest was one of magic and sorcery.
This was followed by a naturalistic polytheism,
which the conquering Semites, less civilized
than those whom they had conquered, adopted
in part, until, about two thousand years before
our era, having won the upper hand, they gradually reduced the primitive gods to the rank
of mere attributes of Baal, the supreme divinity, the sun-god.

These inscriptions, then, have taught us nothing concerning the secret—if there is a secret
—of the Chaldean religion, and have not contributed anything of any value to the information already in our possession, thanks to certain fragments of Berosus, whose accuracy they
have more than once enabled us to verify.

Berosus, as the reader may remember, was a
Chaldean astromer, a priest of Belus in Babylon, who about the year 280 B. C.—shortly,

that, is, after the death of Alexander—wrote
in Greek a history of his country. As he could
read cuneiform characters he was able to profit
by the archives of the temple of Babylon. Unfortunately the work of Berosus is almost entirely lost; all that is left of it is a few fragments collected by Josephus, Eusebius, Tatian,
Pliny, Vitruvius, and Seneca. This loss is all
the more regrettable in that Berosus, who seems
to have been a serious and conscientious historian, declared that he had had access to documents attributed to the beings who preceded
the appearance of man on the earth; and his
history, according to Eusebius, covered 2,150,-
000 years. We have also lost his cosmogony,
and with it all the astronomical and astrologi-
cal science of Chaldea, which was the great
secret of the Babylonian Magi, whose zodiac
dates back 6700 years. We have only the
treatise known as "Observations of Bel," translated into Greek by Berosus, though the
text that has come down to us is of much later
date.

The few pages that are all that is left us of
the Chaldean cosmology contain a sort of anti-
cipation of the Darwinian theories of the origin
of the world and of man. The first god and
the first man were a fish-god and a fish-man
—which is, by the way, confirmed by embry-
ology—born of the vast cosmic ocean; and na-

ture, when she attempted to create, produced at first anomalous monsters unable to reproduce themselves. As for their astrology, according to Professor Sayce, the learned professor of Assyriology at Oxford, it seems to be chiefly based on the axiom, *post hoc ergo propter hoc;* which is to say that when two events occur in sequence the second is regarded as the result of the first; hence the care with which the astrologers used to observe celestial phenomena in order that they might empirically foretell the future.

To sum up, we are very imperfectly acquainted with the official religion of Assyria and Babylonia, whose gods appear to be rather barbaric. This religion does not become more enlightened or more interesting until after the conquest of Cyrus, which brought into the country the Zoroastrian and Hindu doctrines, or confirmed and completed those that had, in all probability, already found their way into the secrecy of the temples; for Chaldea had always been the great crossroads on which the theologies of India, Egypt, and Persia were of necessity wont to meet. Thus it was that these doctrines found their way into the Bible and the cabala, and thence into Christianity.

But as far as the origin of religion is concerned, we must admit that the authentic documents recently discovered teach us virtually nothing, and that all that has been said of the esoterism and the mysteries of Chaldea is based merely upon legends or writings that are notoriously apocryphal.

CHAPTER VI

GREECE BEFORE SOCRATES

I

TO complete this brief survey of the primitive religions—this inquiry into the origins of the Great Secret—we must not overlook the pre-Socratic theogony.

Before the classic period the Greek philosophers, of whose works we possess only mutilated fragments—Pythagoras, Petronius Hippasus, Xenophanes, Anaximander, Anaximenes, Heraclitus, Alcmæon, Parmenides of Elea, Leucippus, Democritus, Empedocles, Anaxagoras, —were already in the ridiculous and uncomfortable situation in which the Hebrew cabalists and the occultists of the middle ages found themselves about fifteen to twenty centuries later. They seem, like the latter, to have had a presentiment of the existence, or the dim tradition, of a religion more ancient and of a nobler character than their own, which had replied, or had endeavored to reply, to all the anxious questions as to divinity, the origin and the purpose of the world, eternal Becoming and impassive Being; the passage from chaos to the cosmos; the emergence from the vast sum of things and the return thereto; spirit and substance, good and evil; the birth of the universe and its end; attraction and repulsion; fate; man's place in the universe and his destiny.

Above all, this lost tradition, which we found in India all but intact, marks once for all the divorce between the knowable and the unknowable; and, attributing the lion's share to the latter, it had the courage to implant in the very heart of its doctrine a tremendous confession of ignorance.

But the Greeks do not seem to have realized the existence of this confession, simple, definite, and profound though it was, albeit it would have saved them a great deal of vain inquiry; or else, their intellect—subtle, more active, more enterprising than ours—was unwilling to admit it; and all their cosmogony, their theogony, and their metaphysics are merely an incessant endeavor to belittle it, by subdividing it, by triturating it ad infinitum, as though they hoped that, by dint of diminishing each separate particle of the unknowable, they would eventually succeed in learning all about it.

What a curious spectacle it is, that of this contest of the Greek intellect—lucid, exacting, fidgety, eager to obtain a clear idea of everything—with the imposing though often extravagant obscurities of the Asiatic religions! It has been said that the Greeks had no conception of the divine Absolute; and this is true, but of a later period. In the beginning their conceptions, as yet under the influence of mysterious traditions, were completely permeated by this sense of the Absolute, which had often led them, by the paths of reason alone, far higher, and perhaps nearer to the truth, than their more capable successors who had lost it.

2

But without speaking in detail of their gropings after a light of which they had some vague intuition, or which was buried deep in the ancestral memory or in myths which were no longer understood; without specifying the contribution of each of the Greek philosophers, which would involve explanations interesting enough but of disproportionate length, we shall merely note the essential points of agreement with the Vedic and Brahman theories.

Xenophanes the first, unlike the poets, affirmed the existence of a sole, immutable, and eternal god. "God," he said, "is not born, for He could not be born save of His like, or of His contrary; two hypotheses of which the first is futile, and the second absurd. One cannot call Him infinite, nor yet finite; for if infinite, having neither middle nor beginning nor end, He would be nothing at all; and if finite He would be encompassed by limitations and would cease to be One. For like reasons He is neither at rest nor in movement. In short, one cannot attribute to Him any characteristics but negative ones." [1] This is really tantamount to admitting, in other words, that He is as unknowable as the First Cause of the Hindus.

This acceptance of the Unknowable is more clearly formulated by Xenophanes in another passage:

"No one understands, no one ever will understand, the truth concerning the gods and the things which I teach. If any one did happen to come upon the absolute truth he would never be aware of the encounter. Nowhere do we find anything more than probability."

Might we not repeat to-day what the founder of the Eleatic school affirmed more than twenty-five centuries ago? Was there, here, as elsewhere, an infiltration of the primitive tradition? It is probable; in any case, the filiation is clearly proved in other particulars. The Orphics whom we find at the legendary and prehistoric source of Hellenic poetry and philosophy were really, according to Herodotus, Egyptians.[2] We have seen, on the other hand, that the Egyptian religion and the Vedic religion have probably a common origin, and

[1] Albert Rivaud, *Le Problème du Devinir;* p. 102.
[2] Herodotus; II, 81.

that it is for the moment impossible to say
which is the more ancient. Now the Pythagoreans borrowed from the Orphics the wanderings of the soul and the series of purifications.
Others have taken from them the myth of
Dionysus, with all its consequences; for Dionysus, the child-god, slain by the Titans, whose
heart Athene saved by hiding it in a basket, and
who was brought to life again by Jupiter, is
Osiris, Krishna, Buddha; he is all the divine
incarnations; he is the god who descends into
or rather manifests himself, in man; he is
Death, temporary and illusory, and rebirth, actual and immortal; he is the temporary union
with the divine that is but the prelude to the
final union, the endless cycle of the eternal
Becoming.

3

Heraclitus, who was regarded as the philosopher of the mysteries, explains the nature of
this cycle. "On the periphery of the circle
the beginning and the end are one." [1] "Divinity is itself," says Auguste Dies, "the origin
and the end of the individual life. Unity is
divided into plurality and plurality is resolved
into unity, but unity and plurality are contem-
poraneous, and the emanation from the
bosom of the divine is accompanied by an

[1] Heraclitus, 102.

incessant return to divinity." [1] All comes from God, all returns to God; all becomes one, one becomes all. God, or the world, is one: the divine idea is diffused through every quarter of the universe. In a word, the system of Heraclitus, like that of the "Vedas" and the Egyptians, is a unitarian pantheism.

In Empedocles, who follows Xenophanes and Parmenides, we find, in the province of cosmology, the Hindu theory of the expansion and contraction of the universe, of the god who breathes it in and breathes it out, of alternative externalization and internalization.

"In the beginning the elements are inextricably mingled in the absolute immobility of the Spheros. But when the force of repulsion, after remaining inactive on the external circumference, has resumed its movement toward the center, separation begins. It would proceed to absolute division and dispersal of the individual, were it not that an opposing force reassembles the scattered elements until the primitive unity is gradually reconstructed." [2]

The Greek genius, of which we have here an interesting example, seeks as far as possible to explain the inexplicable, whereas the Hindu genius contents itself with feeling it as something majestic and awe-inspiring, calls the force of

[1] Auguste Dies, *Le Cycle Mystique;* p. 62.
[2] *Ibid.;* pp. 84–85.

repulsion hatred; the force of attraction, affection. These forces exist from all eternity. "They were, they will be, and never, to my thinking, will unending time contrive to throw them off. Now plurality resolves, by the aid of love, into unity; and now unity, in hatred and strife, divides itself into plurality."

But whence comes this duality in unity? Whence arise the opposing principles of attraction and repulsion, of hatred and love? Empedocles and his school do not tell us. They merely state that in division, repulsion, or hatred there is decadence, but in attraction, in the return to unity and love, there is ascent or reascent; and thus the Hindus referred the idea of decadence or downfall to matter, and the idea of reascension and return to divinity, to the spirit. The confession of ignorance is the same, and so is the means of emerging from hatred and escaping from matter. In the first place there is purification during life, a purification entirely spiritual. "Blessed is he," says the philosopher Agrigentes, "who acquires a treasury of divine ideas; but woe to him who has but a hazy conception of the gods."

Here again and above all we have purification by successive reincarnations. Empedocles goes further than the Vedic religion, which confirms itself—at all events until Manu's time—to the reincarnation of man in man. He, like the

Pythagoreans, accepts metempsychosis: that is, the passing of the soul into animals, and even into plants, whereby it is led by a series of ascents, back to the divinity from which it emerged, and into which it enters and is reabsorbed, as into the Hindu Nirvana.

4

It is perhaps of interest in this respect to note that, as in the Vedic and Egyptian doctrine, there is no question of external rewards and punishments. In the pre-Socratic metempsychosis, as in Hindu reincarnation and before the tribunal of Osiris, the soul judges itself and automatically, so to speak, awards itself the happiness or the misery which is its right. There is no enraged and vengeful deity, no special place of damnation set aside for miscreants, or for expiation. We do not expiate our sins after death, because there is no death. We expiate them only in our lifetime, by our lives: or rather there is no expiation; only the scales fall from our eyes. The soul is happy or unhappy because it does or does not feel that it is in its proper place; because it can or cannot attain the height which it hoped to conquer. It is aware of its divinity only in so far as it has understood or understands God. Stripped of all that was material, all that had blinded it, it perceives itself suddenly on the

farther shore, just as it was, though unknown to itself, on the hither side. Of all its
possessions, of its happiness or its fame, nothing is left but its intellectual and moral acquisitions. For in itself it is nothing more
than the thoughts which have possessed it and
the virtues which it has practised. It sees itself as it is, and catches a glimpse of what it
might have been; and if it is not satisfied it
tells itself, "It must all be done over again";
and of its own free will it returns to life, aim-
ing at a higher mark and reëmerging happier
and of greater stature.

5

On the whole, in the theology and the myths
of the pre-Socratic period, as in the theologies
and the myths of the religions which preceded
them, there is no hell and no heaven. In the
underground caverns of hades, as in the mead-
ows of the Elysian fields, there are only the
phantoms, the astral *manes,* the Egyptian doubles, the inconsistent relics of our discarnate
shades. The instruments of their torment or
the accessories of their pale felicity are but
evidence of identity, by the aid of which, like
the vague interlocutors of our spiritualists,
they seek to make themselves known. Here,
just as in India, hell is not a place but a state

of the soul after death. The *manes* are not chastised in a place of semi-darkness; they simply continue to live there by the reflection of their former lives. There Tantalus is always thirsty; there Sisyphus rolls his rock; there the Danaïdes exhaust themselves in seeking to fill their bottomless measure; there Achilles brandishes his lance, Ulysses bears his oar, and Hercules draws his bow; their vain effigies repeat to infinity the memorable or habitual actions of their lives on earth; but the imperishable spirit, the immortal soul is not there; it is purifying itself elsewhere, in another body; it is advancing upon the long invisible path which leads it back to God.

At this stage, as in all remote beginnings, there is as yet no fear of death and the beyond. This fear does not manifest itself or develop in the great religions until the latter begin to be corrupted for the benefit of priests and kings. The intuition and intelligence of mankind have never again reached the height which they attained when they conceived the ideal of divinity of which we find the most authentic traces in the Vedic traditions. One might say that in those days man disclosed, at the topmost height of his stature, and there established, once for all, that conception of the divine which he subsequently forgot and frequently degraded; but despite oblivion and

ephemeral perversion, its light was never lost.
And that is why we feel, beneath all these
myths, behind all these doctrines, which are
sometimes so contradictory, the same optimism,
or at all events the same ignorant confidence;
for the most ancient secret of mankind is really
a blind, stupendous confidence in the divinity
from which it emerged without ceasing to
form part of it and to which it will one day return.

There are still many points of contact which
might well be singled out; for example, the
atomic theory, which contains some extraordinary instances of intuition. Leucippus and Democritus in particular taught that the gyra-
tory movement of the spheres exists from all
eternity, and Anaxagoras developed the theory
of elemental vortices which the science of our
own days is rediscovering. But what we have
just recorded will doubtless appear sufficient.
For the rest, in this philosophy, which is only
too generally regarded as a tissue of absurdities
and puerile speculations, we are dealing with
most of the great mysteries that perplex humanity. On examining it more closely we find
in it some of the most wonderful efforts of human reason, which, secretly sustained by the
truth contained in certain cloudy myths, approaches the probable and the plausible more
closely than most of our modern theories.

6

We may suppose that the most important parts of this theosophy and philosophy, namely, those which treated of the Supreme Cause and the Unknowable, were gradually neglected and forgotten by the classic theosophy and philosophy, and became, as in Egypt and India, the secret of the hierophants, forming, together with more direct oral traditions, the foundations of the famous Greek mysteries, and notably of the Eleusinian mysteries, whose veil has never been pierced.

Here again the last word of the great secret must have been the confession of an invincible and inviolable ignorance. At all events, whatever negative and unknowable elements may already have existed in the myths and the philosophy of which he was constantly being reminded, they were enough to destroy, for the initiate, the gods adored by the vulgar, while at the same time he came to understand why a doctrine so perilous for those who were not in a position to realize its exalted nature had to remain occult. There was probably no more than this in the supreme revelation, because there is probably no other secret that man might conceive or possess; that there never can have existed, nor ever will exist, a formula that will give us the key of the universe.

The Great Secret

But apart from this confession, which must have seemed overwhelming, or of the nature of a release, in accordance with the quality of the recipient's mind, it is probable that the neophyte was initiated into an occult science of a more positive nature, such as that possessed by the Egyptian and Hindu priests. Above all, he must have been taught the methods of attaining to union with the divine, or to immersion in the divine by means of ecstasy or trance. It is permissible to suppose that this ecstasy was obtained by the aid of hypnotic methods; but these methods were those of a hypnotism far more expert and more fully developed than our own, in which hypnotism properly so called, magnetism, mediumship, spiritualism, and all the mysterious forces—odic and otherwise—of the subconscious self, which were then more fully understood than they are to-day, were commingled and set to work.

The writer whom many persons regard as the greatest theosophist of our day—Rudolph Steiner—professes, as we shall see later on, to have rediscovered the means, or one of the means, of producing this ecstasy, and of placing one's self in communication with higher spheres of existence, and with God.

7

From the foregoing we may, so it seems, conclude that the higher initiates, or, to speak more precisely, the adepts of the esoteric religions, of the colleges of priests or the occult fraternities, did not know very much more concerning the beginning and the end of the universe, the unknowable nature of the First Cause, the father of the gods, and the duties and destinies of mankind, than that which the great primitive religions had taught, openly and to those who were capable of understanding it. They did not know more for the reason that as yet it was not possible to know more, or consequently to teach more. If they had known anything further we too should know it; for it is hardly conceivable that the gist of such a secret should not have transpired if so many thousands of men had known it for so many thousands of years. If it were possible to imagine that such a secret existed and that we could understand it, in understanding it we should no longer be men. There are limits to knowledge which the brain has not yet passed, and which it never will be able to pass without ceasing to be human. At most the confessions of irreducible agnosticism and absolute pantheism, which are the two poles between which the loftiest human thought has always hesitated, is hesitating now, and in all probability will al-

ways hesitate, might have been more definite,
more clearly expressed, less wrapped in formal-
ities, and more complete, and might have put
those who received it on their guard against
the fallacious appearances and the necessary
lies of the official theogonies and mythologies.

8

Still, at a certain level there was no esoteric
cosmogony, theogony, or theology, no secret
code of morality.   In this connection, as we
have just seen, the primitive religions left nothing unexplored; not so much as a shadowy
corner where the lovers of mystery, the investigators of the unknown might take refuge.
Their ethic is from the first—or seems to be
from the first, for we know nothing of the
thousands of years during which it was elabo-
rated—the loftiest and most perfect that any
man could hope to practise.   It has passed
through every ordeal, has attempted and
climbed every mountain in its way.   Where it
has passed—and it has passed everywhere, and
above all over the most rugged pinnacles—
nothing is left to be gleaned. We are still
hundreds of centuries beneath its attainments
on the heights of abregation, good-will, pity,
self-sacrifice, and absolute self-devotion; and
most of all in the search for what Novalis

called "our transcendental me"—that is the divine and eternal part of our being.

As for the sanctions, they too went to the extreme, the utmost that the mind can conceive; for, emanating from the Unknowable, they could not, without contradiction, attribute to this Unknowable any sort of will whatever. They were consequently bound to place within us the rewards and punishments of a system of morality which could only have come into being within us. Here again there was not the least room for any occult doctrine.

There remains the riddle of the origin of evil, the apparent antagonism of spirit and matter, the necessity of sacrifice, pain, and expiation. Here again, under pain of contradiction, the occult tradition could not base anything on the unknowable. It had simply to admit, provisionally, the least material explanation of the esoteric religions, which regard matter and darkness, division and separation, not as evil in themselves, but as transitory states of the one and eternal substance, a phase of the unending flux and reflux of Becoming, from which one should strive to emerge as quickly as might be, in order to attain the spiritual state or phase. In this connection it had not, and of course, could not have had a more satisfying doctrine. In any case no echo of such doctrine has come down to us, and it is probable that it once more contented itself with emphasizing the confusion of its invincible ignorance.

9

Here then are the points—and they are the most important—on which the esoteric doctrine, if there was in the beginning such a doctrine, must necessarily be confounded with the public teaching of the primitive religions if considered fairly near their origin. It is probable, as I have already said, that this teaching did not assume a secret character until very much later, when the official religions were extraordinarily complicated and profoundly corrupted. Esoterism was then but a return to the original purity, just as in Greece the pre-Socratic doctrines—which were, whatever may have been said of them, obviously of Asiatic origin—became the teachings of the mysteries. It is therefore all but certain that the occultists of all times and nations knew as little of them as we do. But there are other spheres in which they seem to have had traditions which the official religions do not appear to have handed down to us, and whose secret the successors of the great adepts of India, Egypt, Persia, Chaldea, and Greece, with the cabalists, the Neoplatonists, the Gnostics, and the Hermetics of the middle ages, have more or less unsuccessfully sought to recover.

This province is that of the unknown forces of nature. We can hardly dispute the fact that the priests of India and Egypt, and the Magi of Persia and Chaldea, had a knowledge of chemistry, physics, astronomy, and medicine which we have undoubtedly surpassed in certain respects, but in others we are perhaps very far from having caught up with them. Without recalling here the blocks of stone weighing 1500 tons, transported by unknown means over enormous distances, or the rocking-stones, masses of rock weighing five hundred tons, which were never native to the soil upon which they now rest, and which date from the prehistoric era of the Atlanteans, it is an undoubted fact that the great pyramid of Cheops, for example, is a sort of stupendous hieroglyph, which, by its dimensions, its proportions, its internal arrangements, and its astronomical orientation, propounds a whole series of riddles of which only the most obvious have hitherto been deciphered. An occult tradition had always affirmed that this pyramid contained essential secrets, but only quite recently has any one begun to discover them. Abbé Moreux, the learned director of the Bourges Observatory, giving a complete summary of the question in his *Enigmes de la Science*,[1] shows us

The Great Secret

that the meridian of the pyramid—the line runing north and south passing through its apex—is the ideal meridian; that is, it is that which crosses the greatest amount of land and the smallest amount of sea, and if we calculate exactly the area of habitable territories, it will be found to divide them into two strictly equal halves. On the other hand, if we multiply the height of the pyramid by one million, we obtain the distance from the earth to the sun, or 198,208,000 kilometers, which is, within about one million kilometers, the distance which modern science has finally adopted, after long research and dangerous expeditions to distant lands, and thanks to the progress of celestial photography.

The well-known astronomer Clark has calculated, from recent measurements, the polar radius of the earth. He makes it 6,356,521 meters. Now this is precisely the cubit of the pyramid-builders, or 0.6336321 meters, multiplied by ten millions. Next, on dividing the side of the pyramid by the cubit used in its construction, we have the length of the sidereal year; that is, the time which the sun requires to return to the same point in the sky. Then, if we multiply the pyramid-builders' inch by one hundred millions, we shall obtain the distance which the earth travels in its orbit

[1] P. 5. *et seq.*

144

in one day of twenty-four hours, the approximation being closer than our modern measures —the yard or the meter—would permit of our making. Lastly, the entrance-passage of the pyramid pointed toward the pole star of the period; it must therefore have been orientated with reference to the precession of the equinoxes, according to which phenomenon the celestial pole returns, coinciding with the same stars, after the lapse of 25,796 years.

We see, then, that, as Abbé Moreaux tells us, "all these conquests of modern science are found in the Great Pyramid in the form of natural dimensions, measured, and always capable of measurement, needing only opportunity to shine forth in broad daylight with the metrical meaning contained in them.

It is impossible to attribute these extraordinary data to mere coincidence. They prove that the Egyptian priests, in geography, mathematics, geometry, and astronomy, possessed knowledge that we are barely beginning to reconquer, and there is nothing to tell us that this enigmatic pyramid does not contain a host of other secrets which we have not yet discovered. But the strangest, most disconcerting fact is that none of the innumerable hieroglyphs that have been deciphered, nothing, indeed, to be found in the whole literature of ancient Egypt, makes any allusion to this ex-

traordinary knowledge. It is obvious even
that the priests sought to conceal it; the sacred
or pyramidal cubit, the key to all scientific measurements and calculations, was not employed
in every-day use; and all this miraculous knowledge, coming whence no one knows, was deliber-
ately and systematically buried in a tomb and
propounded as a riddle or a challenge to the
future centuries. Does not the revelation of
such a mystery, due merely to chance, permit
us to suspect that many other mysteries of various sorts are awaiting the hazard of a similar
revelation, in the same pyramid or in other
monuments or in the sacred writings?

In the meantime it is, after all, highly probable that the Egyptian priests taught the Magi
of Chaldea the secret of what Eliphas Levi
calls "a transcendental pyrotechnics," and that
both were acquainted with electricity and had
means of producing and directing it as yet unknown to us. Pliny, in fact, tells us that
Numa, who was initiated into the mysteries of
the Magi, understood the art of creating and
directing the lightning, and that he success-
fully employed his terrible battery against a
monster known as Volta, which was devastat-
ing the Roman Campagna. Forestalling the
invention of the telephone, the Egyptian priests
were able, we are told, to send instantaneous
messages from temple to temple, no matter

what the distance. For that matter, the Bible testifies to their knowledge and power when it shows them, in the midst of the ten plagues, which were only works of magic, fighting Moses by means of miracles, Moses himself being one of their initiates.

II

But it is more especially in connection with the subconscious, with mysteries of the Unknown Guest, and what we to-day call abnormal psychology; with the astral body, hypnotism, and spiritualism; with the properties of the ether, and of unknown fluids; with odylic medicine, hyper-chemistry, survival, and the knowledge of the future, that they must have possessed secrets to discover which the Hermetics of the middle ages wore themselves out amid their pentacles, their cryptograms, and their books of spells, corrupted and incomprehensible. It is apparently in these regions of occultism that there is something left for us to glean; and it is to them that our metaphysics is turning back, though by other roads.

It is likewise in these obscure regions that the last initiates of India, the heirs to the esoteric traditions, excel us so greatly in knowledge, producing those strange phenomena which cannot always be sufficiently explained by trickery and conjuring, and which astonish the most skeptical, the most suspicious of travelers.

Have they in reserve, as they claim, yet other secrets, notably those that enable them to manipulate certain terrible and irresistible forces, such as the intra-molecular energy, or the formidable and inexhaustible forces of gravitation, or of the ether? This is possible, but less certain. It is rather difficult to understand why, in cases of urgency, when there has been a question of life or death, they have never resorted to them. India, like Egypt, Persia, and Chaldea, has suffered terrible invasions which not only threatened her civilization, destroyed her wealth, burned her sacred books, and massacred her inhabitants, but also attacked her gods, violated her temples, and exterminated her priests. Yet we do not discover that she ever turned a supernatural weapon against her aggressors. It may be objected that because of the enormous expanse of the territories invaded the invasions were never complete; that the last initiates might have fled before them, taking refuge in inaccessible mountains; moreover that as their kingdom was not of this world they did not feel that they had the right to employ their super-terrestial powers, for a fundamental axiom of the highest knowledge forbids its employment in pursuit of material profit; and this too is possible. It is none the less a fact that the British domination of Tibet, and above all the entry into that country of Colonel Young-husband's expedition, struck a very palpable blow at the prestige of their occult knowledge.

12

Until 1904, in fact, the occultists had re-garded Tibet as the last refuge of their sci-ence. In Tibet, according to them, there were vast underground libraries, containing innumer-able books, of which some dated back to the prehistoric times of the Atlanteans; and in these the supreme and immemorial revelations were recorded in tongues known only to a few adepts. In the heart of her lamaseries, swarming with thousands of monks, Tibet maintained a college of superior initiates, at the head of which was the initiate of initiates, the incarnation of God on earth, the dalai-lama.

No European, it was said, had ever violated the sacred territory of Tibet; which, by the way, was not quite correct, for in 1661, in 1715, and in 1719 two or three Jesuits and a few Capuchins had found their way into the country. In 1760 a Dutch traveler made a stay in Lhasa, and in 1813 an Englishman. Then, in 1846, the missionaries Huc and Gabet, disguised as lamas, contrived to slip into the

149

country. But since then, despite many perilous attempts, of which the latest and best known was that of Sven Hedin, no explorer had succeeded in reaching the holy city. One may say, therefore, that of all the countries in the world Tibet was the most mysterious, the most illusive.

On the announcement of the sacrilegious expedition strange happenings were anticipated by the world of occultists. I remember the confidence, the serene certainty with which one of the sincerest and most learned of them told me, early in the year 1904: "They do not know what they are attacking. They are about to provoke, in this place of refuge, the most terrible powers. It is virtually certain that the last of the trans-Himalayan adepts possess the secret of the formidable etheric or sidereal force, the *mash-maket* of the Atlanteans, the irresistible *vril* of which Bulwer-Lytton speaks: that vibratory force which, according to information contained in the 'Astra-Vidya,' can reduce a hundred thousand men and elephants to ashes as easily as it would reduce a dead rat to powder. Extraordinary things are about to happen. They will never reach the inviolable Potala!"

And what happened? Nothing whatever; at least, nothing of what was anticipated. After long diplomatic negotiations, in which the incapacity, unintelligence, senility, and bad faith of the Chinese, and the childish cunning of the college of lamas were revealed in a most disconcerting fashion, Colonel Younghusband's force, consisting chiefly of Sikhs and Gurkhas, proceeded to enter the country. In those rugged regions, the most inhospitable in the world, on the high frozen plateaus of the Himalayas, desolate and uninhabitable, they had to overcome unheard-of difficulties; and in passes which a handful of men, under good leadership, would have rendered unassailable, they were met more than once by the unskilful though courageous resistance of the dalailama's soldiery, filled with fanatical valor by the *mantras* and spells of their priests, but armed with match-locks and inferior native artillery. At length the British force drew near to Lhasa; and for five days the distracted abbots of the great monasteries solemnly cursed the invaders, set thousands of prayer-wheels turning, and resorted to the supreme incantations: all to no avail. On August 9 Colonel Younghusband made his entry into the capital of Tibet, and occupied the holy of holies, the house of God, the Potala; an immense and fantastic structure which soars upwards from the hovels of the city, resembling, with its terraces, its flat roofs, and its buttresses, a fortress, a piled-up mass of Italian

The Great Secret

villas, a barracks with innumerable windows, and certain American sky-scrapers. The dalai-lama, the thirteenth incarnation of divinity, the Buddhist pope, the spiritual father of six hundred millions of souls, had shamefully taken to flight and made good his escape. The convents and sanctuaries, swarming with monks —there were more than thirty thousand of them, indifferent and resigned—were explored; but nothing was found save the relics of the noblest religion ever known to mankind, finally rotting and dwindling into puerile superstitions, mechanical prayer-wheels, and the most deplorable witchcraft. And thus collapsed the final refuge of mystery; thus were surrendered to the profane the ultimate secrets of the earth.

CHAPTER VII

THE GNOSTICS AND THE NEOPLATONISTS

I

LEAVING aside Plato and his school, whose theories are so well known that we need not recall them here, we shall now leave the comparatively limpid waters of the primitive religions to enter the troubled eddies which succeed them. As the simple and awe-inspiring conceptions whose very altitude hid them from view were lost to sight, those which followed them, and were but their shattered or distorted reflections, became more turbid and increased in number. It will suffice to pass them rapidly in review; for to judge by what we know, or rather by what we know that we cannot know, they no longer have very much to teach us, and can but fruitlessly confuse and complicate the confession of the less knowable and the consequences which proceed therefrom.

Before the reading of the hieroglyphs, the discovery of the sacred books of India and Persia, and the labors of our own scientific metapsychologists, the only sources of occultism were the cabala and the writings of the Gnostics and Neoplatonists of Alexandria.

The Great Secret

It is not very easy to locate the cabala chronologically. The "Sefer Yezireh," as we know it, which is as it were the entrance to the cabala, seems to have been written about 829 A. D., and the "Zohar," which is the temple, about the end of the thirteenth century. But many of the doctrines which it teaches go back very much further: namely, to the Babylonian captivity, and even to the bondage of the Israelites in Egypt. From this point of view, then, we must place it before the Gnostics and the Neoplatonists; but on the other hand it has borrowed so much from the latter and they have influenced it so greatly that it is almost impossible to speak of it until we have said something of those to which it owes the best and the worst of its theories.

2

It is true that these Jewish traditions, for their part, mingled their abundant streams with those of the other Oriental religions which from the first century to the sixth invaded the Greek and Roman theosophy and philosophy, causing men to call in question and to examine more closely the beliefs and theories by which they had lived. There was in the intellectual world, and above all in Alexandria, whither flowed all races and all doctrines, a strange force of curiosity, restlessness, and activity. For the first time—at all events, so it is believed—the Hellenic philosophy found itself directly in contact with the Oriental religions and philosophies—audacious, grandiose, unfathomable—which until then it had known only by hearsay or by niggardly fragments. The Gnostics contributed, among other doctrines, those of Zoroaster, while the mysterious Essenes, theosophists and theurgists, who came from the shores of the Dead Sea, and rather mysteriously disappeared (although in the days of Philo they were forty thousand strong) or were eventually absorbed by the Gnostics, doubtless represented the Hindu element more directly; the cabalists, who existed before the cabala was committed to writing, infused fresh life into the doctrines of Persia, Chaldea, and Egypt; the Christians woke up to find themselves between the Bible and the legends of India; and the Neoplatonists, who might more correctly be called the Neo-Orphics or Neo-Pythagoreans, returned to the old philosophers of the sixth century before our era, striving to find in them truths too long ignored, which were suddenly restored to daylight by the revelations from the East.

We need not here investigate this effervescence, which constitutes one of the most intense, and, in some respects, most fruitful crises ever recorded in the history of human thought. For

our present purposes it is enough to note that
from the point of view of the idea of God, of
the First Cause, of the pre-cosmic Spirit, or the
absolute Reality, which precedes all being,
manifest or conditioned, as from the point of
view of the origin, purpose, and economy of
the universe and the nature of good and evil,
it teaches us nothing that we have not found
in previous religions and philosophies. The
manifestations of the Unknowable, the division of the primordial Unity, and the descent
of spirit into substance are attributed to the
Logos; they change their name without lessen-
ing the surrounding darkness. In the attempt
to find an explanation of the insoluble contradictions involved by an impassive god and a
universe in incessant movement, an unknowable
god who is finally known in every detail, a good
god who creates, desires, or permits evil, men
imagined, first, a threefold hypostasis, and
then a host of intermediate divinities, demi-
urges, or reduplications of God, eons, or divine
faculties and attributes personified, angels, and
demons. In the backwaters of these special-
izations, distinctions, and subdivisions, subtle,
ingenious, and inextricable, the simple though
tremendous confession of the Unknowable was
soon submerged by such a tide of words that
it was no longer visible.[1]   Before long it was

[1] The Gnostics taught that the Supreme Being, or Perfect

The Gnostics and the Neoplatonists

completely forgotten, was no longer referred
to; and the Supreme Unknown engendered so
many and so familiar secondary divinities that
it no longer dared to remind men that they
could never know it. Of course the greater
the number of phrases and explanations, the
more completely were the primitive verities, on
which all was founded, effaced and obscured;
so that after men had attained, or regained,
in Philo, and above all in Plotinus, the loftiest
summits of thought, they descended, on the
one hand, to the lucubrations of that Chinese
puzzle, the famous "Pistis-Sophia," attributed
to Valentinian, and on the other to the pretended revelations of Iamblichus concerning
the Egyptian mysteries—revelations which revealed nothing whatever—and the whole Gnostic and Neoplatonic movement ended, with the
successors of Valentinian and those who continued the work of Porphyry and Proclus, by
sinking into the most puerile logomachy and
the most vulgar witchcraft.

We need not, therefore, consider the movement any further: not that the study of this
effervescence would be devoid of interest; on
the contrary, there are few moments of history

Eon, or, as we should say, the Eternal, could be approached
only by a number of emanations or eons. In other words,
these were regarded as eternal Beings who acted as intermediaries between the Perfect Eon and mankind, and, being
joined together formed the Perfect Eon.—TRANS.

157

at which the mind has been forced to encounter problems of so novel, complex, and difficult a nature, or at which it has given proof of greater power, vitality, and enthusiasm. But what I have already said of this period is enough for my purpose, which is merely to show that the occultists of Greece, and, above all, those of the middle ages, who interest us more especially because they are closer to us, so that our memory of them is more vivid, have nothing essential to teach us that we have not already learned from India, Egypt, and Persia.

CHAPTER VIII

THE CABALA

I

WE come at length to the cabala, which is in some sort the vital center of occultism as it is commonly understood.

This word, cabala, which covers doctrines that are in general or very imperfectly understood, is for some enveloped in mystery and illusion of a perturbing nature, at which they all but shudder as though they saw therein a reflection of infernal fires; while for others it evokes merely an unreadable jumble of absurd superstitions, of so much sheer nonsense, of fantastic formulæ that lay claim to satanic powers; childish riddles and obsolete lucubrations which are no longer worthy of serious examination. As a matter of fact the cabala merits neither this excess of honor nor this indignity. To begin with, there are two cabalas: the cabala properly so called, the theoretical cabala, the only one with which we need concern ourselves; and the practical cabala, which is merely a sort of senile dermatosis, that gradually invades the less noble parts of

the first, degenerating into imbecile practices
of black magic and sordid witchcraft, in which
it is impossible to take any interest.

The philosophical, critical, and scientific study
of the cabala, like that of Vedism, of the hieroglyphs, or of Mazdeism, is a thing only of
yesterday. Before Franck published his works
on the subject, the cabala was known only by
Knorr von Rosenroth's volume, the *Kabbala
Denudata,* published in 1677, which, in sur-
veying the "Zohar," examines only the "Book
of Mysteries" and the "Great Assembly"; that
is, its obscurest portions, neglecting the text,
and giving only imperfectly understood extracts
from the commentators. Franck, in his *Kabbala ou la Philosophie Religieuse des Hébreux,*
which appeared in 1842, reproduced the complete and authentic texts for the first time,
translating them and commenting upon them.
Joël and Jellinck continued his researches, discussed his conclusions and corrected his mistakes, and the latest interpreter of these mysterious books, S. Karppe, in his *Étude sur les
Origines et la Nature du Zohar,* returning to
the problem already propounded, and going
back to the sources of Jewish mysticism, gave
us in 1901 a survey which enables us to ad-
venture without fear on this perilous and suspect soil.

The cabala, from the Hebrew *kaballah,*

which, as all the dictionaries will tell you, signifies tradition, claims to be a body of occult doctrine, coincident with or rather complementary to the teaching of the Bible, or the orthodox doctrines of the *Torah,* that is to say, of the Pentateuch, transmitted orally from the time of Moses, who is supposed to have received them directly from God, until a period which extends from the ninth to the thirteenth or fourteenth century of our era, when these secrets, whispered from mouth to ear, as the initiates used to say, were finally set down in writing. It is impossible to know how far this claim is justified, for beyond the first or second century before Christ the historical traces which might connect the tradition that we know with an earlier tradition are absolutely lacking. We must therefore confine ourselves to taking the two volumes of the cabala—the "Sefer Yerizah" and the "Zohar"—as we find them, and consider what they contained at the time when they were written.

The "Sefer Yerizah," or "Book of Creation," which was at first attributed, childishly enough, to the Patriarch Abraham, and then, without certainty, to the Rabbi Akiba, is briefly the work of an unknown author who compiled it in the eighth or ninth century of our era.

To give some idea of this work, it will

suffice to transcribe a few paragraphs of the
first chapter:

"By thirty-two voices of marvelous wisdom
Yah, Yehovah Zebaoth, the living God, God
the All-Highest, abiding forever, whose name is
holy (He is sublime and holy), set forth and
created His world in three books; the Book
properly so called, the Number, and the
Word.

"Ten Sephiroth unassisted, twenty-two
letters of which three are fundamental letters,
seven double letters and twelve simple letters.

"Ten Sephiroth unassisted, conforming with
the number of ten fingers, five facing five. And
the alliance of the One is exactly adapted to
the middle by the circumcision of the tongue
and the circumcision of the flesh.

"Ten Sephiroth unassisted, ten and not nine,
ten and not eleven. Understand with wisdom and meditate with intelligence; examine
them, look into them deeply. Refer the
thing to its light and set its author in his
place.

"Ten Sephiroth unassisted; their measure is
the ten without end: profundity of beginning
and profundity of end; profundity of good
and profundity of evil; profundity of height
and profundity of depth; profundity of east and
profundity of west; profundity of north and
profundity of south; one sole master, God,

faithful King, reigns over all from the height of his holy and eternal dwelling.

"Ten Sephiroth unassisted; their aspect is like the lightning, but their end has no end. His command to them is that they shall hasten and come, and according to His word they hurl themselves forward like the tempest, and prostrate themselves before His throne.

"Ten Sephiroth unassisted; their end fixed to their beginning and their beginning to their end, like a flame attached to the coal. The Master is unique and has no helpers. Now what art thou before the One?"

And so it goes on interminably, plunging into a sort of incomprehensible superstition of letters and numbers considered as abstract powers. It is certain that one can make such texts say anything one pleases, and that one gets out of them anything one wants. We find here for the first time the conception of the Sephiroth, which the "Zohar" will unfold more completely; and we discover in it a system of creation in which "the Word, that is, the Word of God, by expressing the letters *Alef, Mem, Schin,*" as is explained by S. Karppe, one of the most learned commentators of this enigmatic book, "gives birth to the three elements, and producing with these letters six combinations, it gives birth to six directions; that is, it gives the elements the power to extend them-

The Great Secret

selves in all directions. Then, instilling into these elements the twenty-two letters of the alphabet, including the three letters *Alef, Mem,* and *Schin* (no longer as substantial elements, but as letters), and expressing the whole variety of words which result from these letters, it produces the entire multiplicity of things." [1]

All this, as we see, reveals nothing of great importance; and I should not have lingered over these solemn tomfooleries were it not that the "Sefer Yerizah" enjoys a reputation among occultists which hardly seems deserved when one looks into the matter, and serves as a point of departure and a basis for the "Zohar," which constantly refers to it.

The occultists have endeavored to give us the keys of the "Sefer," but I humbly confess that for me these keys have opened nothing. After all, it is probable enough, as Karppe says, that this mysterious volume is merely the work of a pedagogue bent upon concentrating, in a very brief handbook, all the elementary scientific knowledge relating to reading and grammar, cosmology and physics, the division of time and space, anatomy, and Jewish doctrine; and that instead of being the work of a mystic it is rather a sort of encyclopedia, a mnemotechnical enchiridion.

[1] S. Karppe, *Études sur les Origines et la Nature du Zohar;* pp. 159 and 163.

The Cabala

2

The "Zohar"—which means "the light,"—
like the "Sefer Yerizeh," is the fruit of protracted mystical fermentation which goes back
to a period when the "Talmud" was not yet
completed; that is, before the sixth century
of our era, and above all during the period
known as Gaonic. After a somewhat lengthy
eclipse, this mysticism revived about the year
820 A. D., and continued to manifest itself in
the writings of the great Jewish theologians;
Ibn Gabirol, Juda ha Levy, Ibn Ezra, and,
principally, in those of Maimonides. Then
directly preparing for the cabala, comes the
school of Isaac the Blind, which is above all
metaphysical—"an abstraction of the Neoplatonic abstractions," as some one has described it, in which Nachmanides shone with
particular brilliance; then the school of Elea-
zar of Worms, which gave special attention to
the mysteries of letters and numbers; and the
school of Abulafia, which devoted itself to pure
contemplation.

This brings us to the "Zohar," properly so
called. Like the Bible, like the "Vedas," the
"Avesta," and the Egyptian "Book of the
Dead," this is not a homogeneous production
but the result of a slow process of incubation,
the work of numbers of anonymous collabora-

tors, incoherent, disconnected, often contradictory, in which one finds a little of everything, of the best as well as the worst, the loftiest speculations being followed by the most childish and extravagant irrelevances. It is a collection, a storehouse, or rather a bazaar, heaped pell-mell with everything that could not find place in the official religion, as being too audacious, too exalted, too fantastic, or too alien to the Jewish spirit.

It is not easy to determine the date of a work of this kind. Franck, to emphasize its antiquity, refers to its Chaldean form. But a great many rabbis of the middle ages wrote Chaldean Aramaic. It was then maintained that it was the work of a Tanaite, Simon ben Jochai (about 150 A. D.), but nothing confirming his authorship has come to light. We find no certain trace of its existence before the end of the thirteenth century. The most probable theory—and the learned Karppe reached this conclusion after a long and minute discussion of all possible hypotheses—is that Moses de Leon, who lived at the beginning of the fourteenth century, most assuredly took a part in the compilation of the "Zohar"; and, if he was not its principal author, gathered into a single whole a number of mystical fragments, commentaries on the Scriptures—resulting, like so many other works of Jewish literature, from the collaboration of a number of writers. In any case, it is certain that the "Zohar" as we know it is comparatively modern.

3

For the Jehovah of the Bible, the only God, personal, anthropomorphic, the direct Creator of the universe, the "Zohar" substitutes the En-sof: that is, the Infinite; or perhaps we should rather say that it is superposed upon Jehovah, or is presupposed; and the En-sof is also the Ayin, that is, the non-existent, the Ancient of Ancients, the Mystery of Mysteries, the Long Face. The En-sof is God in Himself, as unknowable, as inconceivable, as the Cause without cause or the Supreme Spirit of the "Vedas," of which He is only a replica, modified by the Jewish genius. He is even nearer the non-existent than the Supreme Spirit of the Hindus, for His first manifestation, the first Sephira, the "Crown," is still non-existence; it is the Ayin of the Ayin, the non-existence of non-existence. He is not even called "That," as in India. "When all was still contained in Him," says the "Zohar," "God was the Mystery of Mysteries. He was then without name. The only fitting term for Him would have been the interrogation: Who?" [1]

Of this Deity we can give but negative and

[1] "Zohar"; II, 105.

167

contradictory descriptions. "He is separate, since He is superior to all; and He is not separate. He has a shape, and is shapeless. He has a shape in so far as He establishes the universe, and He has no shape in so far as He is not contained in it." [1]

Before the unfolding of the universe He was not, or was but a question-mark in the void. So here we find at the outset the confession of absolute ignorance, invincible, irreducible. The En-sof is but an unlimited enlargement of the Unknowable; the God of the Bible is absorbed and disappears in a vast abstraction; hence the necessity of secrecy.

But it was necessary to make this inconceivable negation—impenetrable, immobile, and eternal, like the Supreme Cause of the Indian religions—emerge from its non-existence and its immobility and pass from the infinite to the finite, from the invisible to the visible; and it is here that the difficulties begin. God being infinite (that is, filling all things, how, beside the En-sof, the Infinite, is there room for the Sof, the finite? The "Zohar" is evidently embarrassed, and its explanations lead it far from the humble and awe-inspiring simplicity of Hindu theosophy. It is loath to admit its ignorance; it wants to account for everything, and, groping in the Unknowable, it entangles itself

[1] "Zohar"; III, 288-a.

in explanations which are often irreconcilable, and when the ground falls away beneath its feet it has recourse to allegories and metaphors, to mask the impotence of its conceptions or to provide an apparent escape from the dilemma in which it has placed itself. For a moment it asks itself whether it can admit of creation *ex nihilo,* extending to this first act the incomprehensible character of the divinity; then it seems to think better of it and rallies to the doctrine of emanation, which it finds in India, in Zoroastrianism, and in the Neoplatonists. It modifies their doctrine, adapting it to the Jewish genius, and complicates it to the utmost without succeeding in explaining it.

This theory of emanation as expounded in the "Zohar" is indeed strangely obscure, uncertain, and heteroclite, lapsing every moment into anthropomorphism.

To make room for the universe, God, who filled space, concentrated Himself; and in the space left free He irradiated His thought and exteriorized a portion of Himself. This first emanation or irradiation is the first Sephira, "the Crown." It represents the Infinite having moved one step toward the finite, non-existence having taken one step toward existence, the first substance. From this first Sephira, which is still almost non-existence, but a non-existence more accessible to our intelligence, emanate or develop two further Sephiroth: Wisdom, the male principle, and Intelligence, the female principle; that is, on proceeding from the Crown the contraries appear, the first differentiation of things. From the union of Wisdom and Intelligence is born Knowledge; we have thus the pure Idea, Thought exteriorized, and the Voice or Speech which connects the first with the second. This first Trinity of Sephiroth is followed by another: Grace or Splendor, Justice or Severity, and their mediatrix, Beauty. Lastly the Sephiroth, mingling in Beauty, develop yet further, and produce a third group: Victory, Splendor, Foundation; and then the Sephira Empire or Royalty, which brings into existence all the Sephiroth in the visible universe.

The Sephiroth as a whole, moreover, constitute the mysterious Adam Kadmon, the primordial super-man, of whom the occultists will have much to tell us, and who himself represents the universe.

This explanation of the inexplicable, like all explanations of the sort, really explains nothing whatever, and conceals the incomprehensible beneath a flood of ingenious metaphors. Obeying, as previous religions had done, the necessity of building a bridge between the infinite and the finite, between the inconceivable and conception, instead of contenting itself, as

did India, with the renewal or the duplication
of the Supreme Cause, or the Egyptian, Persia,
and Neoplatonic Logos, it multiplies the bridges
by multiplying the intermediaries; but numerous though they be, these ladders none the less
end in the same confession of ignorance. At
all events, this explanation, by concealing this
fresh admission beneath a mountain of images,
has the advantage of relegating to a sort of
inaccessible *in pace* the first confession, the principal and most embarrassing admission, which
places the First Cause and the existence of
God beyond our reach. After the creation of
the Sephiroth and of the universe the En-sof
is generally forgotten; like the That of India
or the Nu of Egypt, it is by preference passed
over in silence; and it is but rarely that questions concerning it are asked. It is too secret,
too mysterious, too incomprehensible even for
a secret and mysterious doctrine like that of
the cabala, and the whole attention is given
solely to the emanations which the imagination
attributes to it and which one seems to know
because they have been given names, virtues,
functions, and attributes: in a word, because
man himself has created them.

4

When did the En-sof begin to project its
emanations? To this question, which India

The Great Secret

answered by the theory of the nights and days of Brahma, without beginning or end, the cabala does not give a very clear reply. "Before God created this world," it says, "He had created a great many worlds, and had caused them to disappear until the thought came to him to create this one."[1] What has become of these vanished worlds? "It is the privilege," replies the cabala, "of the strength of the Supreme King that these worlds, which could not take shape, do not perish; that nothing perishes, even to the breath of His mouth; everything has its place and its destination, and God knows what He does with it. Even the speech of man and the sound of his voice do not lapse into non-existence; everything has its place and its dwelling."[2]

And what of our world? Whither is it going? What is its destiny? The Zohar being a heteroclite production, a very late compilation, its doctrine in this respect is much less definite than that of Brahmanism; but if detached from the illogical and alien elements which often cross or divert its course, it likewise attains the stage of pantheism, and by way of pantheism it achieves the inevitable optimism. The En-sof, the Infinite, is everything; consequently everything is the En-sof. To man-

[1] "Zohar"; III, 61-b.
[2] "Zohar"; II, 100-b.

172

ifest itself, the pure abstraction develops itself by means of intermediaries and, in its goodness voluntarily degrading itself, ends in thought, and in matter, which is the last degradation of thought; and when the Messianic era comes "everything will return into its root as it emerged therefrom." [1]

Man, who in the "Zohar" is the center of the world and its microcosm, may from the moment of his death rejoice in this return to perfection; and his purified soul will receive the kiss of peace which "unites it anew and forever to its root, its principle." [2]

And evil? Evil, in the "Zohar," as in Brahmanism, is matter. "Man, by his victory over evil, triumphs over matter, or rather subordinates the matter within him to a higher vocation; he ennobles matter, making it ascend from the extreme point to which it was relegated to the place of its origin. In him, who is the great consciousness, matter acquires consciousness of the distance that separates it from the Supreme Good, and strives to approach the latter. Through man the darkness aspires toward the light, the multiple toward the single. The whole of nature aspires toward God.

"Through man God remakes Himself, hav-

---

[1] "Zohar"; III, 296.
[2] "Zohar"; I, 68-a.

ing passed through the whole splendid divinity
of living creatures.   Since man is an expression
epitomizing all things, when he has overcome
the evil in himself he has overcome the evil
in all things; he draws with him, as he climbs,
all the lower elements, and his ascent entails
the ascent of the whole cosmos." [1]

But why was evil necessary?   "Why," asks
the "Zohar," "if the soul is of heavenly essence, does it descend upon the earth?"   The
reply to this great problem, which no religion
has given, the "Zohar," in accordance with its
habit when embarrassed, evades by means of
an allegory: "A king sent his son into the country that he might grow strong and sound there
and acquire the necessary knowledge.   After
some time he was informed that his son was
now grown up; that he was a strong, healthy
youth, and that his education was completed.
He then, because he loved him, sent the queen
herself to fetch him and bring him back to the
palace.   In the same way nature bears the
King of the universe a son, the divine Soul, and
the King sends him into the country, that is, the
terrestial universe, in order that he may grow
strong, and gain in nobility and dignity." [2]

The disciples of Rabbi Simon ben Zemach
Durân, one of the great scholars of the

[1] S. Karppe, *op. cit.;* p. 478.
[2] "Zohar"; I, 245.

"Zohar," asked him: "Would it not have been better if man had never been born, rather than that he should be born with the faculty of sinning and angering God?" And the master replied: "By no means, for the universe in its actual form is the best thing in existence. Now, the law is indispensable to the maintenance of this universe, otherwise the universe would be a desert; and man in his turn is indispensable to the law." The disciples understood and said: "Assuredly God did not create the world without cause; the law is indeed the raiment of God; it is that by which He is accessible. Without human virtue, God would be but miserably arrayed. He who does evil soils in his soul the raiment of God, and he who does good puts on the divine splendor." [1] We should indeed be gracious were we more exacting than these obliging and respectful disciples.

Another question of the utmost importance, that of eternal punishment, is likewise evaded. Logically, a pantheistic religion cannot admit that God could chastise and eternally torture a portion of Himself. The "Zohar" certainly says somewhere: "How many souls and spirits are there eternally wandering, who never again behold the courts of heaven?"

But in another section it expressly teaches

[1] "Zohar"; I, 23-a-b.

the doctrine of transmigration; that is, the gradual purification of the soul by means of successive existences; and it bases this doctrine, obviously borrowed from the great religions of an earlier period, on certain passages of the Bible; among others, on Ecclesiastes, Chap. IV, v. 2, in which we read: "Wherefore I praised the dead which are already dead more than the living which are yet alive." "What is meant," asks the "Zohar," "by the dead which are already dead?" They are those who have already died once before this; that is, they were no longer bound on their first pilgrimage through life. Now, it is obvious that the doctrine of a purifying transmigration must necessarily exclude eternal punishment.

5

The "Zohar," then, as I have already stated, is a vast anonymous compilation which, under the pretext of revealing to the initiate the secret meaning of the Bible, and especially of the Pentateuch, decks out in Jewish clothing the confessions of ignorance of the great religions of an earlier period, loading these garments with all the new and complicated adornments provided by the Essenes, the Neoplatonists, the Gnostics, and even the first few centuries of Christianity. Whether it admits the fact or not, it is, in respect of the most important points, plainly agnostic, as is Brahmanism. Like Brahmanism, it is also pantheistic. For the "Zohar" likewise the creation is rather an emanation; evil is matter, division or multiplicity, and good is the return to the spirit and to unity. Lastly, it admits the transmigration of souls and their purification, and therefore Karma, as well as the final absorption into the divine; that is, Nirvana.

It is interesting to note that we have here for the first time—for other statements have not come down to us—an esoteric doctrine proclaiming itself as such; and this doctrine has nothing more to teach us than that which we were taught, without reticence and without mystery—at all events, at the outset,—by the primitive religions. Like the latter, with its wholesale admissions and its expedients, different in form but identical at heart, for passing from non-existence to existence, from the infinite to the finite, from the unknowable to the known, it follows the same rationalistic tradition that strives to explain the inexplicable by plausible hypotheses and inductions, to which we might give another shape and other names, but which, taking them on the whole, we could not, even to-day, perceptibly improve. At most we might be tempted to renounce all explanation whatsoever and extend our confession of ignorance to include the sum total of the origins, the manifestations, and the purposes of life. Perhaps this would be the wisest course.

It shows us that it is highly probable that no secret doctrine ever was or ever could be other than secret; and that the loftiest revelations which we have ever been vouchsafed were always elicited from man by man himself.

The importance assumed by this secret doctrine during the middle ages may readily be imagined. Known only to a few initiates, wrapped up in incomprehensible formulæ and images, whispered "from mouth to ear" in the midst of terrible dangers, it had a subterranean radiance, a sort of gloomy and irresistible fascination. It surveyed the world from a far loftier point of view than that of the Bible, which it regarded as a tissue of allegories behind which was hidden a truth known to it alone; it yielded to mankind, through the thickets of its fantastic and parasitical vegetation, the last echoes of the noble precepts, of human reason at its dawn.

CHAPTER IX

THE ALCHEMISTS

I

ALL the occultism, alchemy, or hermetism of the middle ages proceeds from the cabala and the Alexandrian version of the Bible, with the addition, perhaps, of certain traditions of magical practice which were very widespread in ancient Egypt and Chaldea.

From the theosophical and philosophical portion of this occultism we have nothing to learn. It is merely a distorted reflection, an extremely corrupt and often unrecognizable repetition of what we have already seen and heard. The mysterious paraphernalia with which it surrounds itself, which fascinates and deludes the beholder at the very outset, is merely an indispensable precaution to conceal from the eyes of the church the forbidden statements, perilous and heretical, of which it is full. The occult iconography, the signs, stars, triangles, pentagrams, and pentacles, were at bottom mnemonics, passwords, puns, or conundrums, which allowed confederates to recognize one another and to exchange or publish truths which meant the constant threat of the stake, but which to judge by the explanations which have been offered us, do not and could not conceal anything that does not today seem perfectly admissible and inoffensive.

Alchemy even, which is still the most interesting department of medieval occultism, is after all no more than a camouflage, a sort of screen, behind which the true initiates used to search for the secret of life. "The great task," says Eliphas Levi, "was not, properly speaking, the secret of the transmutation of metals, which was an accessory result, but the universal arcanum of life, the search for the central point of tranformation where light becomes matter and is condensed into a world which contains in itself the principle of movement and of life. . . . It is the fixation of astral light by a sovereign magic of the will." And this leads us to the odic or odylic phenomena of which we shall speak in a later chapter, and puts us on the track of this fixation.

What is more, in the eyes of the higher initiates, the search for gold was only a symbol, concealing the search for the divine and the divine faculties in man; and it was only the inferior alchemists who took literally the cabalistic instructions of their conjuring-books, wore themselves out in the hope of solving problems, and ruined themselves in order to make experiments which nevertheless resulted in the progress of chemistry and in discoveries which in some respects that science has never yet surpassed.

2

On the other hand, people are too ready to suppose that the occultism of the middle ages was preëminently diabolic. The truth is that the initiates did not and could not believe in the devil, since they did not accept the Christian revelation as the church presented it to them. "No demons outside of humanity," was one of the fundamental axioms of the higher occultism. "To attribute what we do not understand to the devil," said Van Helmont, "is the result of unlimited idleness." "One must not give the devil the whole credit," protested Paracelsus.

Devils and evil spirits, fallen angels or the souls of the damned, surrounded by eternal flames, will be found crawling only in the dark corners of black magic or witchcraft. The phantasmagoria of nocturnal revels have too often concealed from us the true occultism, which was, above all, though surrounded by the incessant peril of death and encompassed by hostile shadows, a tentative yet passionate search for truth, or at least for a seeming truth,

for there is nothing else in this world; a truth
which had once shone as a beacon through the
darkness, which was possibly still shining elsewhere, but which was apparently lost, so that
only its precious but shapeless relics were to be
found, mingled with the dense dust of irritating
and disheartening falsehoods, while the highest
talents were wasted in a thankless process of
sifting and selection.

3

To dismiss the question of infernal spirits:
the faithful none the less believed in the existence and intervention of other invisible beings.
They were convinced that the world which escapes our senses is far more densely peopled
than that which we perceive, and that we are
living in the midst of a host of diaphanous yet
attentive and active presences, which as a rule
affect us without our knowledge, but which we
can influence in our turn by a special training
of the will. These invisible beings were not
inhabitants of hell, since for the initiates of
the middle ages, almost as certainly as for the
believers in the great religions in the days when
initiation was not yet necessary, hell was not a
place of torture and malediction but a state of
the soul after death. They were either wandering, disembodied spirits, worth very much
what they had been worth during their life on

earth, or they were the spirits of beings who had not as yet been incarnated. These were known as elementals; they were neutral spirits, indifferent, morally amorphous, devoid of will, doing good or evil according to the will of him who had learned to rule them.

It is incontestable that certain experiments carried out by our spiritualists, notably those in connection with cross-correspondence and posthumous appearances (of which we have almost scientific proof), and certain phenomena of materialization and levitation, compel us to reconsider the plausibility of these theories.

As for the instances of evocation, which often fluctuate between "high" magic and sorcery or black magic, and which in the eyes of the public, occupy, with alchemy and astrology, the three culminating pinnacles of occultism: their solemn paraphernalia, their cabalistic formulæ, and their impressive ritual excepted, they precisely correspond with the more familiar evocations which are practised daily about our turning-tables, or the humble "ouija" or magic mirrors. They correspond also with the manifestations which were obtained, for example, by the celebrated Eusapia Paladino, and which are at the present time being produced, under the strictest "controls," by Madame Bisson's medium; with this difference, that instead of the human phantom expected by those present at a modern séance, the believers of the middle ages thought to see the devil in person; and the devil who haunted their minds appeared to them as they imagined him.

Is autosuggestion responsible for these manifestations, or collective suggestion, or exudation, or the transference or crystallization of spiritualized matter borrowed from the spectators, with which is intermingled some extraterrestrial and unknown element? If it is impossible to distinguish such an element when we are dealing with facts which occur before our eyes, it would be all the more audacious to form a decision in the case of phenomena which occurred some hundreds of years ago and are known to us only through a more or less partial narrative.

4

Lastly, alchemy and astrology, the two remaining pinnacles of occultism, were, in the occultism of the middle ages, second-rate sciences which, from the point of view of the Great Secret, do not offer any novel element, their Greek, Hebrew, and Arab origin being connected with Egypt and Chaldea only by means of apocryphal and comparatively recent writings. Pierre Berthelot, in his work on *Les Origines de l'Alchimie,* has given us a masterly survey of the alchemist's science. He has exhausted the subject, or at least the chemical aspect of it; but his work might perhaps be more complete from the point of view of hyperchemistry or meta-chemistry—or of psychochemistry, which would seem to be no less important. It is likewise greatly to be desired that some great astronomer-philosopher should give us, in a work upon astrology, the pendant of this admirable volume; but hitherto the data have been so scanty that the undertaking would hardly seem to be possible. As much might be done for hermetic medicine, which, for that matter, is connected with alchemy and astrology.

But it is possible that alchemy and astrology, which after all are merely transcendental chemistry and astronomy (professing to transcend matter and the stars in order to arrive at those spiritual and eternal principles which are the essence of the one and control the others), would have no surprises or revelations in store for us if we could go back directly to their Hindu, Egyptian, and Chaldean origins; which has not as yet been practicable, for we have nothing to serve as comparison but the famous Leyden Papyrus, which is merely the memorandum-book of an Egyptian goldsmith, containing formulæ for making alloys, gilding metals, dyeing stuffs purple, and imitating or adulterating gold and silver.

5

Among the medieval occultists, almost all
of whom were alchemists, we shall confine ourselves to recalling the names of Raymond Lully
(thirteenth century), *doctor illuminatus* and
author of the *Ars Magna,* to-day almost unreadable; Nicolas Flamel (fifteenth century),
who according to Berthelot is merely a charlatan pure and simple; Reuchlin; Weigel, Boehme's teacher; Bernardo of Treviso; Basil Val-
entin, whose special subject of investigation
was antimony; the two Isaacs, father and son;
Trithemius, whom Eliphas Levi calls "the
greatest dogmatic magician of the middle
ages," although his famous cryptographical-
works—his *Polygraphia* or his *Steganogra-
phia*—consist of a rather puerile playing upon
words and letters; and his pupil Cornelius
Agrippa, author of *De Occulta Philosophia,*
who simply recapitulates the theories of the
Alexandrian school and, in Eliphas Levi's
words, is no more than "an audacious pro-
faner, fortunately extremely superficial in his
writings." We have still to mention Guillaume Postel, a sixteenth century occultist, who
was acquainted with Greek, Hebrew, and Ara-
bic, was a great traveler, and brought back to
Europe some important Oriental manuscripts;
among others the works of Aboul-Feda, the

The Alchemists

Arab historian of the thirteenth century. "The beloved and upright Guillaume Postel," writes Eliphas Levi, in a letter to Baron Spedalieri, "our father in the Sacred Science, since we owe to him our knowledge of the 'Sepher Yerizah' and the 'Zohar,' would have been the greatest initiate of his century had not ascetic mysticism and enforced celibacy filled his brain with the heady fumes of enthusiasm which sometimes caused his lofty intellect to wander"; a remark, be it said in passing, which might be applied to other hermetists of other times and nations.

After mention of Heinrich Khunrath, Oswald Crollins, etc., we come to the seventeenth century, the earlier years of which were the great period of alchemy, which began to approximate to science properly so called. Gastric juice was discovered by Van Helmont, sulphate of soda and the heavy oils of tar by Glauber, who also had a notion of chlorine, while Kunckel discovered phosphorus.

Were I writing a general history of occultism, instead of merely inquiring what new things we may learn from the last of the adepts, whether they were conscious or not of the occult wisdom whose trial we have followed through the ages, I should have been obliged to linger for a moment over the mysterious Templars, who adopted in part the Jewish traditions and the narratives of the "Talmud," and were followed by the Rosicrucians. I ought also to single out and consider at rather greater length two fantastic and enigmatical figures who dominate and summarize all the occultism of the middle ages; namely, Paracelsus and Jacob Boehme. But when we consider them closely we discover that whatever their pretensions, they did not deduce from an unknown source the revelations which they published and which so perturbed their contemporaries.

Philippus Aureolus Theophrastus Bombastes Von Hohenheim, known as Paracelsus (an approximate translation of Hohenheim), was born in Switzerland in 1493 and died in Salzburg in 1541. He bears the burden of an unjust legend which represents him as a drunkard, a debauchee, a charlatan, and a lunatic. He certainly had many faults, and he seems at times to have been somewhat unbalanced; none the less he remains one of the most extraordinary persons mentioned in history. He was a Neoplatonist and consequently was not ignorant of the Alexandrian writings accessible to the hermetics of his time; but it is probable that during his travels in Turkey and Egypt he was able to obtain a more direct knowledge of certain Asiatic traditions relating to the etheric or astral body upon which he based the whole

of his medical theories. He taught, in fact, in
accordance with the ancient Hindu treatises
which have since then been brought to light
by the theosophists, that our maladies are
caused not by the physical body but by the
etheric or astral body, which corresponds pretty
closely with what to-day is termed the subconsciousness, and, consequently that it was before all necessary to act upon this subconsciousness. Certain it is that many facts in many cir-
circumstances tend to confirm this theory, and it
may be that the therapeutics of to-morrow
will lead us in this direction. According to
Paracelsus, even plants have an etheric body,
and medicaments act not in virtue of their chemical properties, but in virtue of their astral
properties; an hypothesis which would seem to
be corroborated by the comparatively recent
discovery of the "od," which we shall consider
in a later chapter.

His conceptions relating to the existence of a
universal vital fluid, the Akahsa of the Hindus,
which he called the Alkahest, and of the astral
light of the cabalists, are also among those to
which our modern ideas of the preponderant
functions of the ether are calling our attention.
It is obvious, on the other hand, that he often
exceeds all bounds, as when he carries to alto-
gether excessive lengths a childish systematiza-
tion of purely apparent or verbal concordances

between certain portions of the human body
and those of medicinal plants; while his assertions on the subject of the Archai, a species of
special or individual jinnee placed in charge of
the functions of the various organs, and the
fantastic chalatanry of his homunculus are
equally indefensible. But these errors were
inherent in the science of his day and are possibly not much more ridiculous than our own.
When all is said, there remains the memory of
a truly amazing pioneer and a prodigious visionary.

As for Jacob Boehme, the famous cobbler of
Goerlitz, his case would be miraculous and absolutely inexplicable if he had really been the
illiterate that some have called him. But this
legend must decidedly be abandoned. Boehme
had studied the German theosophists, notably
Paracelsus, and was perfectly familiar with the
Neoplatonists, whose doctrines, indeed, he reproduced, recasting them to some extent and
wrapping them up in a more obscure phraseology, which none the less was often unexpected
and extremely impressive; and mingling them
with the elements of the cabala and a certain
amount of mystical mathematics and of alchemy. I refer those who may be interested
in this strange and assuredly brilliant though
very unequal spirit—for his work is full of un-

readable rubbish—to an essay which Emile Boutroux has devoted to him: *Le Philosophe Allemand Jacob Boehme.* They could have no better guide.

CHAPTER X

THE MODERN OCCULTISTS

I

BEFORE the discoveries of the Indianists and Egyptologists, the modern occultists, who—with the exception of Swedenborg, a great isolated visionary—may be counted as descending from Martinez Pasqualis, who was born in 1715 and died in 1779, had perforce to study the same texts and the same traditions, applying themselves, according to taste, to the cabala or to the Alexandrian theories. Pasqualis wrote nothing, but left behind him the legend of an extraordinary magician. His disciple, Claude de Saint-Martin, the "Unknown Philosopher," was a sort of intuitive theosophist, who ended by rediscovering Jacob Boehme. His books, carefully thought out and admirably written, may still be read with pleasure and even with advantage. Without lingering over the Comte de Saint-Germain, who claimed to retain the memory of all his previous existences, Cagliostro, the mighty illusionist and formidable charlatan, the Marquis d'Argens, Dom Pernetty, d'Espréménil, Lavater, Eckartshausen, Delille de Salle, the Abbé Terrasson, Bergasse, Clootz, Court de Gebelin, or all the mystics who toward the end of the eighteenth century were to be found in swarms, in aristocratic circles and the masonic lodges, and were members of the secret societies which were preparing the way for the French Revolution but have nothing of importance to teach us, we may pause for a moment at the name of Fabre d'Olivet, a writer of the first rank, who has given us a new interpretation of the Genesis of Moses, audacious and impressive. Being no Hebrew scholar I am not competent to pronounce upon its value, but the cabala seems to confirm it; and it presents itself surrounded by an imposing scientific and philosophical equipment.

2

And we now come to Eliphas Levi and his books, with their alarming titles: "A History of Magic," "The Key to the Great Mysteries," "Dogma and Ritual of the Higher Magic," "The Great Arcanum, or Occultism Unveiled," etc., the last master of occultism properly so called, of that occultism which immediately precedes that of our metapsychists, who have definitely renounced the cabala, Gnosticism, and the Alexandrians, relying wholly on scientific experiment.

The Great Secret

Eliphas Levi, whose true name was Alphonse-Louis-Constant, was born in 1810 and died in 1875. In a certain sense he epitomized the whole of the occultism of the middle ages, with its fumbling progress, its half-truths, its definitely limited knowledge, its intuitions, its irritating obscurities, its exasperating reticences, its errors and prejudices. Writing before he had the opportunity or the inclination to profit by the principal discoveries of the Egyptologists and the Indianists and the work of contemporary criticism, and himself devoid of all critical spirit, he studied only the medieval documents of which we have spoken; and apart from the "Sepher Yerizah," the "Zohar" (which, for that matter, he knew only from the fantastical fragments in the *Kabbala Denudata*), the "Talmud," and the Book of Revelation, he applied himself by preference to the most undeniably apocryphal of these documents. In addition to those which I have mentioned his three "bedside books" were the "Trismegistus," and "The Tarot."

The "Book of Enoch," attributed by legend to the patriarch Enoch, the son of Jared and the father of Methuselah, must actually be assigned to a date not far removed from the beginning of the Christian era, since the latest event with which its author was acquainted was the war of Antiochus Sidetes against John Hyrcanus. It is an apocalyptic book, probably from the pen of an Essene, as is proved by his angelology, which exerted a profound influence over Jewish mysticism before the advent of the "Zohar."

The "Writings of Hermes Trismegistus," translated by Louis Ménard, who devoted an authoritative essay to the text, is attributed to Thoth, the Egyptian Hermes, and reveals some extremely interesting analogies with the sacred books of India, and notably with the "Bhagavata-Gita," demonstrating once again the universal infiltration of the great primitive religion. But chronologically there is not the slightest doubt that the birthplace of the "Poimandres," "The Asclepius," and the fragments of the "Sacred Book," was Alexandria. The Hermetic theology is full of Neoplatonic and other expressions and ideas, borrowed from Philo, and whose passages of the "Poimandres" may be compared with the Revelation of St. John, which they actually echo, proving that the two works were written at periods by no means distant from one another. It is therefore not surprising that as far as the religion of ancient Egypt is concerned they have no more to teach us than had Iamblichus, since at the period when the Greeks investigated it the symbolism of this religion, as Louis Ménard has observed, was already a dead letter to its very priests.

As for the "Tarot," it is, according to the occultists, the first book written by human hand and earlier than the sacred books of India, whence it is supposed to have made its way into Egypt. Unfortunately no trace of it has been discovered in the archæology of these two countries. It is true that an Italian chronicle informs us that the first card game, which was merely a vulgarized form of the "Tarot," was imported into Viterbo in 1379 by the Saracens, which betrays its Oriental origin. At all events, in its present form it does not go back further than Jacquemin Gringonneur, an illuminator in the reign of Charles VI.

It is obvious that with such data Eliphas Levi could not have any very important revelations to make us. He was moreover embarrassed by the ungrateful and impossible task which he had set himself in endeavoring to reconcile occultism with Catholic dogma. But his scholarship in his own province is remarkable; and he often displays amazing intuition, in which he seems to have come within sight of more than one discovery claimed by our metapsychists, notably in anything relating to mediums, the odic fluid, the manifestations of the astral body, etc. Further, when he deals with a subject which is not purely chimerical and is connected with profound realities—morality, for example, or even politics—and when he does not, as so many occultists do, wrap himself up in wearisome implications which seem afraid of saying too much, though in reality they betray only the fear of having nothing at all to say, he sometimes contrives to write admirable passages, which, after the exaggerated repute which they used to enjoy, do not deserve the unjust oblivion to which they are apparently condemned to-day.

3

Of the school of Eliphas Levi, and following almost the same track, we may reckon two considerable writers; Stanislas de Guaita and Dr. Encausse, better known by the name of Papus. Theirs is a rather special case. Two eminent scholars, they have a profound knowledge of cabalistic and Greco-Egyptian literature, and all the Hermetism of the middle ages. They are likewise familiar with the works of the Orientalists, the Egyptologists, and the theosophists and the purely scientific investigations of our occultists. They know also that the texts upon which they rely are apocryphal and of the most doubtful character; and although they know this, and from time to time proclaim it, yet they start from these texts as a basis; they

The Great Secret

hold fast to them; they confine themselves to them, building their theories upon them, as though they were dealing with authentic and unassailable documents. Thus de Guaita builds up the most important part of his work on the "Emerald Table," an apocryphal work of the apocryphal Trismegistus, having first declared: "We shall not quarrel over the authenticity, authorship, or date of one of the most authoritative initiatory documents that have been handed down to us from Greco-Egyptian antiquity.

"Some persist in seeing in it merely the nonsensical work of some Alexandrian dreamer, while others claim that it is an apocryphal production of the fifth century. Some insist that it is four thousand years older.

"But what does that matter? One thing is certain; that this page sums up the traditions of ancient Egypt." [1]

It is not by any means certain, seeing that the authentic monuments of the Egypt of the Pharaohs offer us absolutely nothing to confirm this mysterious summary, and the writer's "What does that matter?" is rather startling, referring as it does to the text which he has made the keystone of his doctrine.

Papus, for his part, devotes a whole volume of commentary to the "Tarot," in which he sees

[1] Stanislas de Guaita, *La Clef de la Magie Noire;* p. 119.

the most ancient monument of esoteric wisdom, although he knows better than anybody that no authentic traces of it are to be found before the fourteenth century.

In calling attention to this fantastic fault at the base of their work—and it naturally has many ramifications,—I have no intention of questioning the integrity, the evident good faith of this extremely interesting work, which is full of original views, of ingenious intuitions, hypotheses, interpretations, and comparisons, of careful research and interesting discoveries. Both writers know many things which have been forgotten or neglected but which it is well sometimes to recall, and if Papus too often works hastily and carelessly, de Guaita is always mindful, almost to excess, of his careful, dignified, polished, and rather formal phrasing.

4

The position of the new theosophists is to some extent analogous with that of the three occultists of whom I have just been speaking. We know that the Theosophical Society was founded in 1875 by Madame Blavatzky. I need not here pass judgment on this enigmatical woman from the ethical point of view. It is undoubtedly the fact that the report of Dr.

The Great Secret

Hodgson, who was sent out to India in 1884 by the Society for Psychical Research especially to conduct an inquiry into her case, reveals her in a somewhat unfavorable light. Nevertheless, after considering the documentary evidence, I must admit that it is after all quite possible that the highly respectable Dr. Hodgson may himself have been the victim of trickery more diabolical than that which he believed himself to have unmasked. I know that extensive plagiarism has been imputed to Madame Blavatzky and other theosophists; in particular it is claimed that Sinnet's "Esoteric Buddhism" and "The Secret Doctrine" are the work of one Palma, whose manuscripts are supposed to have been bought by the founders of the Theosophical Society, that they contain unacknowledged passages, barely disguised, from works which had appeared twenty years earlier over the signature of various European occultists, and notably that of Louis Lucas.

I shall not linger over these questions, for they seem to me far less important than that of the secret and prehistoric documents and esoteric commentaries upon which the whole theosophical revelation is founded. Whoever the author or authors may be, I shall consider their work as it is presented. "Isis Unveiled," "The Secret Doctrine," and the rest of Madame Bla-

vatzky's very numerous works form a stupendous and ill-balanced monument, or rather a
sort of colossal builder's yard, into which the
highest wisdom, the widest and most exceptional scholarship, the most dubious odds and
ends of science, legend and history, the most
impressive and most unfounded hypotheses, the
most precise and most improbable statements
of fact, the most plausible and most chimerical
ideas, the noblest dreams, and the most incoherent fancies are poured pell-mell by inexhaustible truck-loads. There is in this accumulation of materials a considerable amount of
waste and fantastic assertions which one re-
jects a priori; but it must be admitted, if we in-
tend to be impartial, that we also find there
speculations which must rank with the most
impressive ever conceived. Their basis is evidently Vedic, or rather Brahman and Vedan-
tic, and is to be found in texts that have nothing occult about them. But upon the texts of
the official Indianists the Theosophists have
superimposed others, which they claim are
purer and much more ancient, and which were
provided and expounded by Hindu adepts, the
direct inheritors of the immemorial and secret
wisdom. It is certainly a fact that their writings, without revealing anything new as regards
the essential points of that great confession of
ignorance which bounds the horizon of the

ancient religions, none the less provide us with a host of explanations, commentaries, theories, and details which would be extremely interesting if only they had been subjected, before they were offered to us, to a historical and philological criticism as strict as that to which those Indianists who do not profess to be initiates have subjected their documents. Unfortunately this is not the case. Let us take, for example, the "Book of Dzyan"; that is, the mysterious *slocas* or stanzas which form the basis of the whole secret doctrine taught by Madame Blavatsky. It is represented as being "an archaic manuscript, a collection of split palm-leaves, rendered, by some unknown process, invulnerable to water, air, or fire, and written in a lost language, in *Sinzar,* earlier than Sanskrit, and understood only by a few Hindu adepts"— and that is all. Not a word to tell us where this manuscript comes from; how it has been miraculously preserved; what *Sinzar* is; to which of the hundred languages, which of the five or six hundred Hindu dialects, it is related; how it is written; how it can still be understood and translated; what is approximately the period from which it dates, etc. No attention has been paid to these details. It is always so. One must believe a bare statement, without investigation. These methods are obviously deplorable, for if the texts in question had been sifted by an adequate process of criticism they would be among the most interesting in Asiatic literature. Such as they are offered to us, the Cosmogony and the anthropogenesis of the "Book of Dzyan" appear to be the speculations of Brahmans and might form part of the "Upanishads." An ingenious commentary accompanies them, the work of adepts absolutely familiar with the progress of Western knowledge. If they are really authentic prehistoric documents, their statements as to the evolution of the worlds and of man, partly confirmed as they are by our latest discoveries and scientific theories, are truly sensational. If they are not what they profess to be, their assertions are mere hypotheses, still impressive and sometimes plausible, but usually incredible and needlessly complicated, and, in any case, arbitrary and chimerical.

5

This does not alter the fact that "The Secret Doctrine" is a sort of stupendous encyclopedia of esoteric knowledge, above all as regards its appendices, its commentaries, its *parerga,* in which we shall find a host of ingenious and interesting comparisons between the teachings and the manifestations of occultism throughout the centuries and in different countries. Sometimes there flashes from it an un-

expected light whose far-spreading rays illumi-
nate regions of thought which are rarely fre-
quented to-day. In any case, the work would
prove once again, if proof were needed, and
with unexampled lucidity, the common origin
of the conceptions which were formed by the
human race, long before history as we know it,
of the great mysteries which encompassed it.
We also find in it some excellent and comprehensive tabulations in which occult knowledge
is confronted by modern science and often
seems, as we must admit, to outstrip or excel
the latter. Many other things, too, we find in
it, thrown together at random, but by no means
deserving the contempt with which we have for
some time professed to regard them.

However, it is not for me to write the history of theosophy, or to judge it. I have
simply noted it in passing, since it is the penulti-
mate form of occultism. It will suffice to add
that the defects of its original method have
been emphasized and aggravated by Madame
Blavatzky's successors. With Mrs. Annie Be-
sant—a remarkable woman in other respects—
and with Leadbeater, everything is in the air;
they build only in the clouds, and their gratui-
tous assertions, incapable of proof, seem to
rain down thicker and thicker on every page.
Moreover, they seem to be leading theosophy

into the paths along which their early converts
hesitate to follow them.

These defects are especially aggravated and
revealed in all their ingenuousness by certain
writers of the second ranks, less skilful than
their masters in concealing them; for example,
in the work of Scott-Elliot, the historian of
"Atlantis" and "The Lost Lemuria." Scott-
Elliot begins his history of Atlantis in the most
rational and scientific manner. He refers to
historical texts which scarcely permit us to
doubt that a vast island, one of whose extremi-
ties lay not far from the Pillars of Hercules,
sank into the ocean and was lost forever, carry-
ing with it the wonderful civilization of which
it was the home. He corroborates these texts
by carefully chosen proofs derived from sub-
marine orography, geology, chorography, the
persistence of the Sargasso Sea, etc. Then
suddenly, almost without warning, referring to
occult documents, to charts drawn on baked
clay and miraculously recovered, to revelations
of unknown origin, and to astral negatives
which he claims were obtained in despite of
time and space, and discusses as though they
were on the same footing as historical and geo-
graphical evidence, he describes for us, in all
particulars, as though he were living in their
midst, the cities, temples, and palaces of the

The Great Secret

Atlanteans and the whole of their political, moral, religious, and scientific civilization, including in his book a series of detailed maps of fabulous continents—Hyperborean, Lemurian, etc.—which disappeared 800,000 or 200,000 or 60,000 years ago, and are here outlined with as much minuteness and assurance as though the draftsman were dealing with the contemporary geography of Brittany or Normandy.

6

The head of an independent or dissident branch of theosophy, a scholar, a philosopher, and a most interesting visionary, of whom I have already spoken—Rudolph Steiner,—employs almost the same methods; but he does at least attempt to explain them and justify them.

Unlike the orthodox theosophists, he is by no means content with revealing, discussing, and interpreting the secret and sacred books of the Oriental tradition; he is able to find in himself all the truths contained in these books. "It is in the soul," he declares, "that the meaning of the universe is revealed." The secret of all things is within us, since everything is within us, and it is as much in us as it was in Christ. "The Logos, in unceasing evolution, in millions of human personalities, was diverted

206

to and concentered by the Christian conception in the unique personality of Jesus. The divine energy dispersed throughout the world was gathered together in a single individual. According to this conception Jesus is the only man to become God. He takes upon himself the deification of all humanity. We seek in Him what we had previously sought in our own souls." [1]

This search, too long interrupted by the symbol of Christ, must be resumed. This idea, quite defensible if we regard it as the search for the "transcendental ego," of which the subconsciousness of our metapsychists is merely the most accessible portion, becomes much more debatable in the developments which our author attributes to it. He professes to reveal to us the means of awakening, infallibly and almost mechanically, the God that slumbers within us. According to him, "the difference between the Oriental initiation and the Occidental lies in this, that the first is effected in the sleeping state and the second in the waking state. Consequently the separation of the etheric body from the physical body, always dangerous, is avoided." To obtain a state of trance which enables the initiate to communicate with higher worlds, or with all the worlds

[1] Rudolph Steiner. *Le Mystère Chrétien et les Mystères Antiques,* Trans. Edouard Schurè; p. 228.

dispersed through space and time, and even with the divinity, he must, by means of spiritual exercises, methodically cultivate and develop certain organs of the astral body by which we see and hear, in men and in things, entities that never appear on the physical plane. The principles of these exercises, at least as regards their spiritual portions, are evidently borrowed from the immemorial practices of the Hindu Yoga, and in particular from the "Sutra of Patânjali." Thus Steiner tells us that the astral organ which is supposed to lie in the neighborhood of the larynx enables us to see the thoughts of other men and to throw a searching glance into the true laws of natural phenomena. Similarly an organ supposed to lie near the heart is said to be the instrument which serves to inform us of the mental states of others. Whosoever has developed this will be enabled to verify the existence of certain deep-seated energies in plants and animals. In the same way the sense supposed to have its seat in the pit of the stomach is said to perceive the faculties and talents of men and also to detect the part which animals, vegetables, stones, metals, and atmospheric phenomena play in the economy of nature. All this he explains minutely at great length, with all that relates to the development, training, and organization of the etheric body, and the vision of the Higher

The Modern Occultists

Self, in a volume entitled "Initiation, or the Knowledge of the Higher World." [1]

When we read this dissertation on the state of trance, which is, by the way, a remarkable work from more than one point of view, we are tempted to ask whether the author has succeeded in avoiding the danger against which he warns his disciples: whether he has not found himself "in a world created in every detail by his own imagination." Moreover, I do not know whether experiment confirms his assertions. It is possible to test them. His methods are simple enough, and, unlike those of the Yoga, perfectly inoffensive. But the spiritual training must take place under the direction of a master, who is not always easy to find. In any case, it is permissible to conceive of a sort of "secondary state," possessing advantages over that of the hypnotic subject or the somnambulist or the medium, which would be productive of visions or intuitions very different from those afforded us by our senses or our intelligence in their normal state. As for knowing whether these visions or intuitions correspond with realities on another plane or in other worlds, this is a question which can be dealt with only by those who have experienced them. Most of the great mystics have had

[1] Rudolph Steiner, *L'Initiation,* Trans. Jules Sauerwein; pp. 188 *et seq.*

visions or intuitions of this kind spontaneously; but they do not possess any real interest unless it can be proved that they are experienced by mystics who are truly and absolutely illiterate. Such, it is maintained, were Jacob Boehme, the cobbler theosophist of Goerlitz, and Ruysbroeck l'Admirable, the old Flemish monk who lived in the thirteenth and fourteenth centuries. If their revelations really contain no unconscious reminiscences of what they have read, we find in them so many analogies with the teaching, which later become esoteric, of the great primitive religions, that we should be compelled to believe that at the very roots of humanity, or at its topmost height, this teaching exists, identical, latent, and unchangeable, corresponding with some objective and universal truth. We find, notably, in Ruysbroeck's "Ornament of the Spiritual Espousals," in his "Book of the Supreme Truth," and his "Book of the Kingdom of Lovers," whole pages which, if we suppress the Christian phraseology, might have been written by an anchorite of the early Brahmanic period or a Neoplatonist of Alexandria. On the other hand, the fundamental idea of Boehme's work is the Neoplatonic conception of an unconscious divinity, or a divine "nothingness," which gradually becomes conscious by objectifying itself and realizing its latent virtualities. But

The Modern Occultists

Boehme, as we have seen, was by no means an illiterate. As for Ruysbroeck, although his work is written in the Flemish patois which is still spoken by the peasantry of Brabant and Flanders, we must not forget that before he became a hermit in the forest of Soignes he had been a vicar in Brussels and had lived in the mystical atmosphere created, in the thirteenth and fourteenth centuries, by Albert the Great, especially by his contemporaries, Johann Eckhart, whose mystical pantheism is analogous with that of the Alexandrian philosophers, and Jean Tauler, who, according to Surius, the translator and biographer of Ruysbroeck, visited the latter in his solitude at Groenendael. Now, Jean Tauler likewise spoke of the union of the soul with the divine and the creation of God within the soul. It will therefore be evident that it is more than a little risky to assert that his visions were perfectly spontaneous.

7

As for Steiner, in his case the question does not arise. Before he found or thought to find in himself the esoteric truths which he revealed, he was perfectly familiar with all the literature of mysticism, so that his visions were provided merely by the ebb and flow of his conscious or subconscious memory. After all, he scarcely differs from the orthodox theosophists, except upon one point, which may appear more or less essential; instead of making, not Buddha, but Buddhas—that is, a succession of revealers or intermediaries—the centers of spiritual evolution, he attributes the leading part in this evolution to Christ, synthesizing in Him all the divinity distributed among men, thus making Him the supreme symbol of humanity seeking the God Who slumbers in its soul. This is a defensible opinion if we regard it, as he appears to do, from the allegorical standpoint, but it would be very difficult to maintain it from the historical point of view.

Steiner applied his intuitive methods, which amount to a species of transcendental psychometry, to reconstituting the history of Atlantis and revealing to us what is happening in the sun, the moon, and the other planets. He describes the successive transformations of the entities which will become men, and he does so with such assurance that we ask ourselves, having followed him with interest through preliminaries which denote an extremely well-balanced, logical, and comprehensive mind, whether he has suddenly gone mad, or if we are dealing with a hoaxer or with a genuine clairvoyant. Doubtfully we remind ourselves that the subconsciousness, which has already surprised us so often, may perhaps have in store for us yet further surprises which may be as fantastic as those of the Austrian theosophist; and, having learned prudence from experience, we refrain from condemning him without appeal.

When all is taken into account we realize once more, as we lay his works aside, what we realized after reading most of the other mystics; that what he calls "the great drama of the knowledge which the ancients used to perform and to live in their temples," of which the life, death, and resurrection of Christ, as of Osiris and Krishna, is only a symbolic interpretation, should rather be called the great drama of essential and invincible ignorance.

CHAPTER XI

THE METAPSYCHISTS

I

WE come now to the occultists of to-day, who are no longer hierophants, adepts, initiates, or seers, but mere investigators applying to the study of abnormal phenomena the methods of experimental science. These phenomena may be noted on every hand by any one who displays a little vigilance. Are they exclusively due to the unknown powers of the subconsciousness, or to invisible entities which are not, are not yet, or are no longer human? Herein resides the great interest, one might say the whole interest, of the problem; but the solution is still uncertain, although the tendency to look for it in another world than ours is becoming more marked; and the conversion to spiritualism of scientists pure and simple, such as Sir Oliver Lodge or, more recently, Professor W. J. Crawford, is not without significance in this respect.

I shall not return in these pages to the spirit messages, the phantasms of the living and the dead, the phenomena of premonition, or the psychometric and mediumistic manifestations of which I gave a brief survey in "Death" and "The Unknown Guest." What I said in these volumes will give the reader a summary and provisional—for in this domain all is provisional—yet a sufficient idea of the present state of metapsychical knowledge in this connection.

There are, however, other factors, which did not then fall within the scope of my work, but with which I must deal to-day: first, because having surveyed, quickly but as completely as is possible in a necessarily brief monograph, the occultism of the past, it is only fair to treat the occultism of the present day in a similar fashion; but also and especially because the points which I then passed over throw a somewhat unexpected light on a number of other factors, and justify us, if not in forming conclusions, at least in drawing certain inferences which will complete this survey.

2

Our modern occultists no longer seek, as did their more presumptuous predecessors, to question the unknowable directly, to go back to the origin of the Cause without a cause, to explain the inexplicable transition from the infinite to the finite, from the unknowable to the known, from spirit to matter, from good

to evil, from the absolute to the relative, from
the eternal to the ephemeral, from the invisible
to the visible, from immobility to movement,
and from the virtual to the actual; and to find
in all these incomprehensible things a theogony,
a cosmogony, a religion, and a morality a little
less hopeless than the obscurity whence man
has striven to draw them.

Having learned wisdom from innumerable
disappointments, they have resigned themselves to a more modest function. In the
heart of a science which by the very nature of
its investigation has almost inevitably become
materialistic, they have patiently conquered a
little island on which they give asylum to phenomena which the laws, or rather the habits of
matter, as we believe ourselves to know them,
are not sufficient to explain. They have thus
gradually succeeded, if not in proving, yet in
preparing us to accept the proof, that there is
in man, whom we may regard as a sort of summary of the universe, a spiritual power other
than that which proceeds from his organs or
his material and conscious mind; which does
not entirely depend on the existence of his
body. We must admit that the island thus
won by our occultists, who are now assuming
the name of metapsychists, is as yet in considerable disorder. One sees upon it all the con-

fusion of a recent and provisional settlement. Thither day by day the conquerors bear their discoveries, great or small, unloading them and heaping them pell-mell upon the beach. There the doubtful will be found beside the indisputable, the excellent by the worthless, while the beginning is confounded with the end. It would seem to be time to deduce, from this abundance and confusion of materials, a few general laws which would introduce a little order into their midst; but it is doubtful whether this could be attempted at the present moment, for the inventory is not yet complete, and one feels that an unexpected discovery may call the whole position in question and upset the most carefully constructed theories.

In the meanwhile one might try to begin at the beginning. Since the phenomena recorded tend to prove that the spiritual power which emanates from man does not entirely depend on his brain and his bodily life, it would be logical to show, in the first place, that thought may exist without a brain, and did, as a matter of fact, exist before there was such an organ as the brain. If one could do this, then survival after death and all the phenomena attributed to the subconsciousness would become almost natural and, at all events, far more capable of explanation.

3

The great objection which the materialists have always brought against the spiritualists, and which they still advance, though to-day with less assurance than of old, may be summed up in these words: "No thought without a brain." The mind or soul is a secretion of the cerebral tissues; when the brain dies thought ceases, and nothing is left.

To this formidable objection, to these statements, apparently irrefutable, since our daily experience of the dead is continually confirming them, the occultists have not hitherto been able to oppose any really serious argument.

They were, at bottom, far more defenseless than they dared to admit. But for some years now the investigations of our metapsychists, from which we have not as yet deduced all the consequences, have provided us, if not with unanswerable arguments, which it may be we shall never find, at least with the raw material which will enable us to hold our own against the materialists; no longer amid the clouds of religion or metaphysics, but on their own territory, whose sole ruler is the goddess—the highly respectable goddess—of the experimental method. Thus above the centuries we once more assemble the affirmations and declarations bequeathed to us by our prehistoric an-

The Metapsychists

cestors as a secret treasure, or one too long buried in oblivion.

We should be thankful enough to avoid these rather useless discussions between the spiritualists and the materialists, but the latter compel us to return to them by blindly maintaining that matter is everything; that it is the source of everything; that everything begins and ends in matter and through matter, and that nothing else exists. It would be more reasonable to admit once for all that matter and spirit are fundamentally merely two different states of a single substance, or rather of the same eternal energy. This is what the primitive religion of India has always affirmed, more definitely than any other cult, adding that the spirit was the primordial state of this substance or energy, and that matter is merely the result of a manifestation, a condensation, or a degradation of spirit. The whole of its cosmogony, theosophy, and morality proceed from this fundamental principle, whose consequences, even though in appearance they amount to no more than a verbal dispute, are in actual fact stupendous.

Thus, to begin with, we must know whether spirit preceded matter, or whether the reverse was the case; whether matter is a state of spirit, or whether, on the contrary, spirit is a state of matter. In the present condition of science, disregarding the teaching of the great religions, is it possible to answer this question?

Our materialists assert that life is the indispensable condition without which it is impossible for thought to rise and take shape in the mind. They are right; but what, in their eyes, is life, if not a manifestation of matter, which already is no longer matter as we understand it, and which we have a perfect right to call spirit, soul, or even God, if we so desire? If they maintain that matter is powerless to produce life unless a germ coming from without calls it into existence, they ipso facto enter our camp, since they acknowledge that something more than matter is needed to produce life. If, on the other hand, they claim that life is an emanation from matter, they are confessing that it was previously contained in matter, and again they find themselves in our ranks. For the rest, they have recently been compelled to admit—see, among others, the experiments of Dr. Gustave le Bon—that no such thing exists as inert matter, and that a pebble, a lump of lava, sterilized by the fiercest of infernal fires, is endowed with an intramolecular activity which is absolutely fantastic, expending, in its internal vortices, an energy which would be capable of hauling whole railway trains round and round the globe. Now what is this activity, this energy, if not an undeniable form of the universal life? And here again we are in agreement. But we are not in agreement when they claim, without reason, or rather against all reason, that matter existed before this energy. We may admit that it has existed simultaneously, from the beginning of the world; but mere logic and observation of the facts compel us to admit that when matter sets itself in motion, when it proceeds to evolve, not internally, as in a pebble, but externally, as in a crystal, a plant, or an animal, it is precisely the energy, the motive-power that was contained in it, that has now determined this movement or this development. This same logic, this same observation of the facts, forces us yet again to acknowledge that when matter is transformed or organized it is not the matter that begins the process, but the life contained in it. Now in this case, as in the disputes that are settled in the courts of law, it is extremely important to know which side began. If it was matter that began—but let us ask, in passing, how it could begin, how it could possibly take the initiative, without ceasing to be matter defined by the material- ists; that is, a thing that is in itself necessarily lifeless and motionless—but if, after all, to admit the impossible, it was matter that be- gan, it is probable enough our spiritual part will perish, or rather will be extinguished with

matter, and will revert, contained in matter, to
that elemental intramolecular activity which
marked its beginning and will mark its end.
If, on the other hand, it was spirit that began, it is no less probable that, having been
able to transform and organize matter, it is
more powerful than matter, and of a different
nature; and that having been able to make use
of matter, to profit by it in the process of evolution, improving and uplifting itself—and the
evolution, which, upon this earth of ours, began
with minerals and ends in man, is assuredly a
spiritual evolution,—it is, I repeat, no less probable that spirit, having shown itself able to
make use of matter and being its master, will
refuse to allow matter, when it seems on the
point of disintegration, to involve it in its material dissolution; that spirit will refuse to accept extinction, when matter becomes extinct;
nor will it lapse into that obscure intramolecular activity whence it drew matter in the beginning.

4

In any case, the question for us has a peculiar interest—as to whether thought preceded
the brain, or whether thought is possible without a brain—this question is determined by
the facts. Before the appearance of man and
the more intelligent of the animals, nature was

already far more intelligent than we are and had already brought into the world of plants, fish, lizards, and reptilian birds, and above all into the world of insects, most of those marvelous inventions which even to-day fill us with an ecstasy of wonder. Where in those days was the mind of nature? Probably in matter, and above all outside matter; everywhere and nowhere, just as it is to-day. It is useless to object that all this was done gradually, with infinite slowness, by means of incessant groping; that goes without saying, but time has nothing to do with the matter. It is therefore obvious, unless you believe that the effect may precede the cause, that there was somewhere, no one knows where, an intelligence which was already at work, although without organs that could be seen or localized; thus proving that the organs which we believe to be indispensable to the existence of an idea are merely the products of a preëxisting idea, the results of a previous and a spiritual cause.

5

In the meantime it is quite possible that since the formation of the human mind nature thinks better than of old. It is quite possible, as certain biologists have claimed, that nature profits by our mental acquisitions, which are poured into the common fund of the universal mind. For my part I see no objection to this, for it does not in the least mean that nature depends for her conceptions on the human mind. She had them all long before we existed. When man invents, say, the printing-press or the typewriter to facilitate the diffusion of his ideas, this does not prove that he needed either invention in order to think.

It seems, indeed, that nature, at least on our little planet, has grown wiser and no longer permits the stupendous blunders of which she used to be guilty, in creating thousands of anomalous monsters incapable of survival. None the less it is true that she did not await our advent before proceeding to think, before imagining a far greater profusion of things than we shall ever imagine. We have not ceased, nor shall we soon cease, to help ourselves with overflowing hands from the stupendous treasury of intelligence accumulated by her before our coming. Ernst Kapp, in his *Philosophie de la Technique,* has brilliantly demonstrated that all our inventions, all our machinery, are merely organic projections, that is, unconscious imitations, of models provided by nature. Our pumps are derived from the animal heart; our cranks and connecting-rods are reproductions of our joints and limbs; our cameras are an adaptation of the human eye; our telegraphic systems, of our nervous system; in the X-rays we have that organic property of somnambulistic clairvoyance which is able to see through opaque substances; which can read, for example, the contents of a letter that has been sealed and enclosed in a threefold metal box. In wireless telegraphy we are following the hints afforded by telepathy, that is, the direct communication of an idea by means of psychic waves analogous to the Hertzian waves; and in the phenomena of levitation and the moving of objects without contact we have yet another indication which we have not hitherto been able to turn to account. It puts us upon the track of methods which will perhaps one day enable us to overcome the terrible laws of gravitation which chain us to the earth, for it seems as though these laws, instead of being, as was supposed, forever incomprehensible and impenetrable, are principally magnetic; that is to say, tractable and utilizable.

6

And I am speaking here only of the restricted world of man. What if we were to enumerate all nature's inventions in the insect world, where she seems to have lavished, long before our arrival on the earth, a genius more varied and more abundant than that which she has expended upon us? Apart from the conception of political and social organizations, which some day we may perhaps imitate, we find in the world of insects mechanical miracles which are beyond our attainments and secret forces of which we have as yet no conception. Consider the Languedocian scorpion: whence does she draw that mysterious aliment which, despite her incessant activity, enables her to live for nine months without any sort of nourishment? Where, again, do the young of the Lycosa of the Clotho spider obtain their food, They, too, possess a similar capacity. And by virtue of what alchemy does the egg of a beetle, the *Minotaurus typhoeus,* increase its volume tenfold, although nothing can reach it from the outside world? Fabre, the great entomologist, without a suspicion that he was repeating a fundamental theory of Paracelsus— for science, despite itself, draws daily closer to magic,—had a shrewd suspicion "that they borrow part of their activity from the energies encompassing them—heat, electricity, light, or other various modes of a single agent," which is precisely the universal or astral agent, the cosmic, etheric, or vital fluid, the Akahsa of the occultists, or the od of our modern theorists.

7

It may be said, in passing, that mindless nature has once more plainly shown our minds

The Metapsychists

the path to follow should they seek to rid us
of the burdensome and repugnant dependence
upon food, which allows us barely a few hours'
leisure between the three or four meals that we
are obliged to consume daily. It may be that
the time is less remote than we suppose when
we shall cease to be greedy stomachs and in-
satiable bellies; when we in our turn shall have
solved the magnificent secret of these insects;
when we, like them, shall succeed in. absorbing
vitality from the universal and invisible fluid
by which not they alone but we ourselves are
surrounded and permeated.

Here is a field that to our human science
is unexplored and unbounded. Here, above all
from the point of view of our spiritual life, is
a transformation which would singularly facilitate our understanding of our future existence; for when we no longer have to make the
three or four meals which now, according to
temperament, encumber or brighten the hours
between sunrise and sunset, we shall perhaps
begin to understand that our thoughts and feelings will not necessarily be unhappy, unoccupied,
distracted, and a prey to eternal tedium when
our day no longer contains the landmarks or
objectives now furnished by breakfast, lunch,
tea, and dinner. It would be an excellent initiation into the diet which will be ours beyond
the tomb and in eternity.

The Great Secret

Returning once more to the problem of thought without a brain, which is the keystone of the whole building: let us suppose that after a cataclysm, such as the earth must assuredly have experienced already, and such as may at any moment be repeated, every living brain, and even the most elementary, the most gelatinous attempt at a nervous or cerebral organization, from that of the amœba to that of man, were suddenly destroyed. Do you believe that the earth would remain bare, uninhabited, inert, and forever lifeless, if the conditions of life were once more to become precisely what they had been before the catastrophe? Such a supposition is scarcely permissible. On the contrary, it is all but certain that life, finding itself surrounded by the same favorable circumstances, would begin all over again in almost the same fashion. Mind would once more gradually come into being; ideas and emotions would reappear, would make themselves new organs, thereby giving us irrefragable proof that thought was not dead, that it cannot die, that somewhere it finds a refuge and continues to exist, intangible and imperishable, above the absolите destruction of its instruments or its media; that it is, in a word, independent of matter.

The Metapsychists

Let us now examine this preëxistence of the mind or spirit in ourselves. Had we already a brain when, at the moment of our conception, we were still no more than the sperm-cell which only the microscope renders visible to the eyes? Yet we were already potentially all that we are to-day. Not only were we ourselves, with our character, our innate ideas, our virtues and vices, and all that our brain, which as yet had no existence, would develop a great deal later; already we held within us all that our ancestors had been; we bore within us all that they had acquired during a tale of centuries whose number no one knows; their experience, their wisdom, their habits, their defects and qualities, and the consequences of their imperfections and their merits; all this was packed, struggling and fructifying, into one invisible speck. And we likewise bore within us (which seems to be much more extraordinary, although it is equally indisputable) the whole of our descendants; the whole unbroken sequence of our children and our children's children, in whom we shall live again through the infinity of the ages, though already we hold within us all their aptitudes, all their destinies, all their future. When matter accumulates so many things in a scrap of filament so fine that it all but escapes the microscope, is it not subtle to the point of bearing a strange resemblance to a spiritual principle?

We shall disregard for the moment the action of our descendants upon ourselves, our characters, and our tendencies; an influence which is probable enough, since they do incontestably exist within us, but which it would take us too long to investigate: and let us for a moment lay stress upon the fact that our ancestors, who to us seemed dead, are continuing in a very real sense to live on in us. I shall not linger over this point, since I wish to consider more recent arguments. I shall therefore content myself with calling your attention to it; for the phenomena of heredity are now recognized and classified. It is an indubitable fact that each of us is merely a sort of sum total of his forebears, reproducing more or less exactly the personality of one or several of them, who are obviously continuing to think and act in him. They think with our brains, you will say. That may be true. They employ the organs at their disposal; but it is evident that they still exist; that they live and think, although they have no brain of their own; and this for the moment is all that we need establish.

9

We have just seen, though our survey was all too brief and too summary, that it is possible for thought to exist without a brain; that it seems anterior to matter and actually exists independent of matter. For the moment I shall note only one of the objections put forward by the materialists. "If thought is independent of matter," they say, "how is it that it ceases to function, or functions only in an incomplete manner, when the brain is injured?" This objection, which, by the way, does not envisage the source of thought, but only the state of its conductor or condenser, loses some part of its value if we oppose to it a sufficient number of observations which prove precisely the contrary. I could, if we had the leisure, place before you a list of cases, vouched for by medical observers, in which thought continued to function normally though the whole brain almost was reduced to pulp or was merely a purulent abscess. I refer those whom this question interests to the works of the specialists; in particular they will find in Dr. Geley's authoritative volume; *De l'Inconscient au Conscient,* [1] some examples which will convince them.

Fundamentally the objection advanced by the materalists is a sophism, which has been ad-

[1] P. 8 *et seq.*

mirably refuted by Dr. Karl von Prel. To say
that every injury to the brain affects the mind,
that all thought ceases when the brain is destroyed, and that the mind is consequently a
product of the brain, is to argue precisely as
who should say that any injury to a telegraphic
apparatus garbles the message; that if the wire
is cut the message no longer exists; therefore
the apparatus produces the message, and no
scientist can possibly imagine that there is an
operator behind the apparatus.

10

We shall now consider the statements which
the scientists have been collecting during the
last few years, collating, over a dividing space
of hundreds and thousands of years, the affirmations of the ancient religions and those of
the occultists. These throw a new light on the
problem. They corroborate, in short, by experiment, the esoteric doctrines in respect of
the astral or etheric body—or the Unknown
Guest, if you prefer it;—in respect of its extraordinary and incomprehensible faculties, its
probable survival, and its independence of our
physical body.

We all knew that a very considerable portion
of our life, of our personality, lay buried in
the darkness of the unconscious or the subconscious. In this darkness we housed the whole

of our organic life: that of the stomach, the heart, the lungs, the kidneys, and even the brain; and there they did their work, in an obscurity never pierced by a ray of consciousness save by chance; in illness, for example. There, too, we lodged our instincts, the lowest and the highest alike; with all that was mysterious, innate and irresistible in our knowledge, our aspirations, our tastes, our capacities, our temperaments, and many other things which we have no time to examine.

But for some years now the scientific investigation of hypnotism and mediumship has enormously enlarged and illuminated this extraordinary and magical domain of the unconscious.

We have come, step by step, to establish the fact, in an objective, material and indubitable fashion, that our little conscious cerebral life is as nothing compared with the vast ultra-cerebral and secret life which we live simultaneously; for this unknown life contains the past and the future, and even in the present can project itself to enormous distances from our physical body. In particular we have ascertained that the restricted, unreliable, and unstable memory which we thought unique is duplicated in the darkness by another memory which is unrestricted, indefatigable, inexhaustible, incorruptible, unshakable, and infallible, recording somewhere, perhaps in the brain, but

in any case not in the brain as we know it and
as it controls our consciousness—for it seems
to be independent of the condition of this
brain,—recording indelibly the most trivial
events, the slightest emotions, the most fugi-
tive thoughts of our lives. Thus, to cite only
one example from among a thousand, a ser-
vant who was absolutely illiterate was able, in
the hypnotic state, to repeat without a mis-
take whole pages of Sanskrit, having some
years earlier heard her first employer, who was
an Orientalist, reading passages from the "Vedas."

It has thus been proved that every chapter
of every one of the thousands of books that
we have read remains indelibly photographed
on the tablets of our memory and may, at a
given moment, reappear before our eyes without the loss of a period or a comma. Thus
again Colonel de Rochas, in his experiments on
the retrogression of the memory and the personality, made his subjects go back over the
whole course of their lives, down to their very
early childhood, whose least details were re-
suscitated with an extraordinary distinctness
and perspective; details which, when they were
verified, were acknowledged to be absolutely
correct. He did even better than this: he succeeded in arousing the memory of their previous lives. But here, verification being more

difficult, his experiments are hardly to the point; and I wish to lead you only on to the firm ground of established and undisputed facts.

II

Well, then, here is an enormous part of ourselves which escapes us; of whose life we know nothing; of which we make no use; which lives and records and acts outside our conscious minds; an ideal memory, which is, practically speaking, of no use to us; by the side of which the memory that obeys us is no more than a restricted summit, a sort of pinnacle, incessantly abraded by time, emerging from the ocean of oblivion, beneath which spreads away, downward and outward, a huge mountain of unchangeable memories, by which the brain is unable to profit. Now on what do we base our personality, the nature of our ego, the identity which above all things we fear to lose by death? Entirely on our conscious memory, for we know no other; and this memory, compared with the other, is, as we have seen, precarious and insignificant. Is it not time to ask ourselves where our ego really exists, where our true personality resides? Is it in the restricted, uncertain, precarious memory or in the spacious, infallible, and unshakable one? Which self should we choose after death? That which consists only of hesitating reminiscences, or the other, which represents the whole man, with no solution of continuity; which has not let slip a single action or spectacle or sensation of our lifetime, and retains, living within it, the self of all those who have died before us? While there is reason to fear that the first memory, that of which our brain makes use, is impaired or extinguished at the moment of death, just as it is impaired or diminished by the least ill-health during life, is it not, on the other hand, more probable that the other more capacious memory, which no shock, no sickness can confuse, will resist the terrific shock of death; and is there not a very good chance that we shall find it intact beyond the grave?

If this is not so, why this stupendous work of registration, this incredible accumulation of unused photographs—for in ordinary life we never even wipe the dust from them—when the few landmarks of our cerebral memory are enough to maintain the essential outlines of our identity? It is admitted that nature has made nothing useless; we must therefore suppose that these pictures will be of use later on, that elsewhere they will be necessary; and where can this elsewhere be, save in another life?

The inevitable objection will be made that it is the brain alone which registers the images and phrases of this memory, just as it registers the images and phrases of the other memory, and that when the brain is dead, etc. There may be some force in this objection; but would it not be more than a little strange were the brain unaided to perform, with a care which would completely absorb it, all these operations, which do not concern it, which it disregards a moment later, and of which it does not seem to have any clear conception? In any case this is not the brain as we commonly understand it, and here already we have a very important admission.

12

But this hidden memory, this cryptomnesia, as the specialists have called it, is only one of the aspects of cryptopsychics, or the hidden psychology of the unconscious. I have no time to recapitulate here all that the scholar, the scientist, the artist, and the mathematician owe to the collaboration of the subconscious. We have all profited more or less by this mysterious collaboration.

This subconscious self, this unfamiliar personality, which I have elsewhere called the Unknown Guest, which lives and acts on its own initiative, apart from the conscious life of the brain, represents not only our entire past life, which its memory crystallizes as part of an integral whole; it also has a presentiment of our future, which it often discerns and reveals; for truthful predictions on the part of certain specially endowed "sensitives" or somnambulistic subjects, in respect of personal details, are so plentiful that it is hardly possible any longer to deny the existence of this prophetic faculty. In time accordingly the subconscious self enormously overflows our small conscious ego, which dwells on the narrow table-land of the present; in space likewise it overflows it in a no less astonishing degree. Crossing the oceans and the mountains, covering hundreds of miles in a second, it warns us of the death or the misfortune which has befallen or is threatening a friend or relative at the other side of the world.

As to this point, there is no longer the slightest doubt; and, owing to the verification of thousands of such instances, we need no longer make the reservations which have just been made in respect of predictions of the future.

This unknown and probably colossal guest—though we need not measure him to-day, having only to verify his existence—is, for the rest, much less a new personality than a personality which has been forgotten since the recrudescence of our positive sciences. Our various religions know more of it than we do; and it matters little whether they call it soul, spirit, etheric body, astral body, or divine spark; for this guest of ours is always the same transcendental entity which includes our brain and our conscious ego; which probably existed before this conscious ego, and is quite as likely to survive it as to precede it; and without which it would be impossible to explain three fourths of the essential phenomena of our lives.

13

Passing over for the moment some of the other properties of this singular personality, which we believed to be forever relegated to invisibility, together with materialization, ideoplasty, levitation, lucidity, bilocation, psychometry, etc., it remains for me to explain in what a curious and unexpected fashion a somewhat recent science has succeeded in recording, investigating, and analyzing some of these physical manifestations, and to inquire how far these observations increase the probabilities of the survival or the immortality of the identical personality, which after all may very well be the essential and imperishable portion of our ego.

I have just explained how far the investigation of hypnotism and mediumship has enlarged the field of the subconscious. Hitherto, in accordance with the school to which the investigator belonged, the phenomena established have been attributed either to sugges-

The Great Secret

tion, or to a fluid of unknown nature, examination having as yet been confined to recording their amazing results. Matters were in this position, and the disputes between the "suggestionists" and the "mesmerists" were threatening to become permanent, when about fifty years ago—to be exact, in 1886 and 1867—an Austrian scientist, Baron von Reichenbach, published his first papers on "odic emanations." Dr. Karl von Prel, a German scientist, completed Reichenbach's work, and, being gifted with a scientific mind of the first order, and intuitive powers which often amounted to genius, he was able to deduce all its consequences. These two writers have not yet had full justice done to them, and their works have not yet obtained the reputation which they deserve. We need not be surprised by this; for the progress of official science, the only science that permeates the public, is always a much more leisurely affair than that of independent science. It was more than a century before Volta's electricity became our modern electricity and the ruler of the industrial world. More than a century, too, had passed since the experiments of Mesmer before hypnotism was finally acknowledged by the medical academies, investigated at the universities, and classed as a branch of therapeutics. It may be as long before Reichenbach's experiments, improved by von Prel and completed by De Rochas, begin to bear fruit. In the meantime their investigations throw an abundant light on a whole series of obscure and confused phenomena whose objective existence they have been the first to prove, while indicating their source.

Reichenbach really rediscovered the universal vital fluid, which is none other than the Akahsa of the prehistoric religions, the Telesma of Hermes, the living fire of Zoroaster, the generative fire of Heraclitus, the astral light of the cabala, the Alkahest of Paracelsus, the vital spirit of the occultists, and the vital force of St. Thomas. He called it "od," from a Sankrit word whose meaning is "that which penetrates everywhere," and he saw in it quite correctly the extreme limit of our analysis of man, the point where the line of demarcation between soul and body disappears, so that it seems that the secret quintessence of man must be "odic."

I cannot, of course, describe in these pages the innumerable experiments of Reichenbach, von Prel, and de Rochas. It is enough to say that in principle the od is the magnetic or vital fluid which at every moment of our existence emanates from every part of our being in uninterrupted vibrations. In the normal state these emanations or effluvia, whose existence was suspected, thanks to the phenomena of hypnotism,

The Great Secret

are absolutely unknown to us and invisible.
Reichenbach was the first to discover that "sensitives"—that is to say, subjects in a state of
hypnosis—could see these effluvia quite dis-
tinctly in the darkness.   As the result of a very
great number of experiments, from which every
possibility of conscious or unconscious suggestion was carefully eliminated, he was able to
prove that the strength and volume of these
emanations varied in accordance with the emotions, the state of mind, or the health of those
who produced them; that those proceeding from
the right side of the body are always bluish in
color, while those from the left side are of
a reddish yellow.   He also states that similar
emanations proceed not only from human beings, animals, and plants, but even from minerals.   He succeeded in photographing the od
emanating from rock crystal; the od given off
by human beings; the od resulting from chemical operations; the od from amorphous lumps
of metal, and that produced by noise or fric-
tion; in a word, he proved that magnetism, or
od, exists throughout nature—a doctrine which
has always been taught by the occultists of
all countries and all ages.[1]

[1] Some recent experiments by Mr. W. J. Kilner, described
in his book, "The Human Atmosphere," give positive proof
of the existence of these emanations, .these effluvia, this
human "aura," or at least of a similar aura which constitutes a true astral or etheric double.   It is enough to look
at the subject through a screen formed of a very flat glass

14

Here then we have the existence of this universal emanation experimentally demonstrated. Now let us inquire into its properties and effects.

I shall confine myself to a few essential facts. Thanks to these emanations it has been possible to prove that this fluid is the same as that which produces the manifestations of table-turning; in the eyes of a sensitive, indeed, these manifestations are accompanied by luminous phenomena whose synchronism leaves no doubt that the emission of the fluid is correlated with the movements of the table. The latter does not move until the radiations proceeding from the hands of those experimenting have become sufficiently powerful. These radiations condense into luminous columns over the center of the table, and the more intense they become the more lively is the table. When they fade away the table falls back motionless.

It is the same with the displacement of ob-

dish containing an alcoholic solution of dicyanin, a coal-tar derivative which makes the retina sensitive to the ultra-violet rays; and the aura becomes visible not only to sensitives, as in Reichenbach's experiments, but also in the eyes of 95 per cent. of persons possessed of normal vision. It is, however, possible that this aura is not an etheric double, but a mere nervous radiation. In this connection, see the excellent summary by Monsieur René Sudre in No 3 of the *Bulletin de l'Institut Metapsychique International* (January–February, 1921).

jects without contact, levitation, and so forth: manifestations which to-day are so far established and verified that there is no need to repeat their occurrence. It is therefore an established fact that this fluid, which is able to set in motion a pendulum in a glass vase hermetically sealed with the blow-pipe, just as it is capable of lifting a table weighing more than two hundred pounds, possesses a power which at times is enormous and is independent of our muscles. This power may be attributed to our nerves, our minds, or what not, but is no less plainly and purely spiritual in its nature.

Moreover it is almost certain, although the experimental proofs are in this case less complete and more difficult, on account of the scarcity of subjects, that it is the same odic or odylic force that intervenes in the phenomena of materialization; notably in those produced by the celebrated Eusapia Paladino and by Madame Bisson, which latter are far more conclusive and far more strictly controlled by the medium. It probably draws, either from the medium or from the spectator, the plastic substance with whose help it fashions and organizes the *tangible* bodies which are called into existence and disappear in the course of these manifestations, thereby giving us a very curious glimpse of the manner in which thought, spirit, or the creative fluid acts upon matter, concentrating and shaping it, and how it sets about the business of creating our own bodies.

15

It has further been experimentally demonstrated that this odic or odylic fluid may be conveyed from place to place. Any material object may be filled with it. The object magnetized, into which the hypnotist has poured some porion of his vital energy, all possibility of suggestion being set aside, will always retain the same influence over the sensitive or medium; that is, the influence desired by the hypnotist. It will make the medium laugh or weep, shiver or perspire, dance or slumber, according to the purpose of the hypnotist when he emitted the vital fluid. Moreover, the fluid appears to be indestructible. A marble pestle, magnetized and placed successively in hydrochloric, nitric, and sulphuric acids and subjected to the corrosive action of ammonia, loses nothing of its power. An iron bar heated to a white heat, resin melted and solidified in a different shape, water that has been boiled, paper burned and reduced to ashes, all retain their power. Further—to prove that the detection of this force is not dependent on human impressions—it has been shown that water which has been magnetized and then boiled causes the needle of a rheostat —an instrument for measuring electric currents—to deviate through an angle of twenty degrees, just as it did before it was boiled. It would be interesting to know whether this vital force, thus imprisoned in a material object, can survive the hypnotist. I do not know whether any experiments have been made in respect of this detail. In any case, it has been observed that more than six months after they were charged with od, the most miscellaneous substances—iron, tin, resin, wax, sulphur, and marble retained their magnetic powers intact.

16

Not only does the odic fluid thus transferred contain and reproduce the will of the hypnotist; it also contains and represents part of the personality of the hypnotic subject and in particular his sensitiveness to impressions. Colonel de Rochas has conducted, in connection with this phenomenon, which he calls "the externalization of sensibility," a host of experiments, bewildering yet unassailable and conclusive, which lead us straight back to the magical practices of the wizards of antiquity and the sorcerers of the middle ages, which shows us once more that the most fantastic beliefs or superstitions, provided they are sufficiently general, almost always contain a hidden or forgotten truth.

I need not refer the reader of these pages to experiments which are familiar to all those

who have ever glanced through a volume dealing with metapsychics. I must keep within certain bounds; and what I have said is enough
to establish the fact that there is within us a
vital principle which is not indissolubly bound
up with the body, but is able to leave it, to
externalize itself, or at least in part, and for a
brief period, during our lifetime. It may be
rendered visible; it possesses a power independent of our muscles; it is able to condense matter, to shape it, to organize it, to make it live,
not merely in appearance, like phantoms of the
imagination, but like actual tangible bodies,
whose substance evaporates and returns to us in
the most inexplicable fashion. We have also
seen that this vital principle may be transferred to a given object, and there, despite all
physical and chemical treatment of the object,
it will maintain, indestructibly, the will of the
hypnotist and the sensibility of the hypnotized
subject. May we not at this point ask ourselves whether, being to this extent separable
from and independent of the body—whether being so far indestructible, as, for example, in the
ashes of a burned document, which contained
only a very small portion of it—whether this
vital fluid does not survive the destruction of
the body? In reply to this question we have,
quite apart from logic, the extremely impressive
evidence of those learned societies which have

devoted themselves to the investigation of
strictly authenticated cases of survival; and, in
particular, the 500 to 600 apparitions of the
dead verified by the Society for Psychical Research. It must be admitted that these apparitions, which are probably odic manifestations
from beyond the grave, seem far more credible
when we are acquainted with certain properties
of the mysterious fluid which we have been
considering.

17

Since the death of the leaders of the "odic"
school—Reichenbach, von Prel, and de Rochas,
—the investigation of the magnetic or odic
fluid has been somewhat neglected; mistakenly,
to our thinking, for it was by no means exhaust-
ive; but there are fashions in metapsychics as
in everything else. The Society for Psychical
Research, in particular, during the last few
years, has devoted itself almost exclusively to
the problems of "cross correspondences"; and
while its inquiry has not yielded absolutely unassailable results, it does at least permit us to believe more and more seriously in the presence
all about us of spiritual entities, invisible and
intelligent; disembodied or other spirits, who
amuse themselves—the word is employed ad-
visedly—by proving to us that they make nothing of space or time and are pursuing some
purpose which we cannot as yet understand.   I

know, of course, that we can, strictly speaking, attribute these unexpected communications to the unknown faculties of the subconsciousness; but this hypothesis becomes daily more precarious, and it may be that the time is not far distant when we shall be finally compelled to admit the existence of these disembodied entities, "doubles," wandering spirits, "elementals," "Dzyan-Choans," devas, cosmic spirits, which the occultists of old never doubted.

In this connection, to say nothing for the present of Sir Oliver Lodge's *Raymond,* or of the highly interesting spiritualistic experiments of P. E. Cornillier, or of a host of other experiments the consideration of which would take us too far afield, the recent researches of Dr. W. Crawford, which have made a sensation in the world of metapsychics, have afforded a remarkable confirmation of the theory of the "invisibles." It is true, however, as we shall see, that this confirmation proceeds less from the facts themselves than from the interpretation which has been placed upon them.

18

W. J. Crawford, a doctor of science and a professor in Belfast University, has of late undertaken a series of experiments in connection with "telekinesia," or movements without contact; experiments which were conducted with a degree of scientific precision that vholly excluded any idea of fraud, and which absolutely confirm those which Crookes, the *Institut Psychologique,* and Ochorovicz carried out with Home, Eusapia Paladino, and Mademoiselle Tomscyk as mediums.

The subject of these experiments was that most peculiar phenomenon which is a sort of physical externalization; of the duplication, amorphous at first, and afterward more or less plastic, of the medium. From the medium's body proceeds an indefinable substance, which is sometimes visible, as in the case of Eva, Madame Bisson's medium, and sometimes invisible, as in the case of Crawford's medium, but which, even though invisible, may be touched and measured, and behaves as though it possessed an objective reality.

This substance, moist, cold and, sometimes viscous, which is known as "ectoplasm" can be weighed, and its weight exactly corresponds with the weight lost by the medium; and it may attain as much as 50 per cent. of the medium's normal weight.

In these experiments this invisible substance behaves as though it emerged from the medium's body in the form of a more or less rigid stem, which lifts a table placed at a certain distance from the chair in which the medium is seated. If the table is too heavy to be lifted

The Metapsychists

directly at arm's length, so to speak, the psychic stem or lever curves itself, chooses a fulcrum on the floor, and erects itself to lift the weight. When this invisible lever has its fulcrum in the medium's body the weight of the latter is increased by that of the object lifted: but when it selects a fulcrum on the floor the medium's weight is diminished by the pressure exerted on the floor.

These phenomena of levitation were perfectly well known before Dr. Crawford's investigation; but by his discovery of the invisible lever, sometimes perceptible to the touch and even capable of being photographed, he is the first to reveal the entire material and psychical mechanism. Moreover in the course of his innumerable experiments he noted that everything happened as though invisible entities were watching the experiments, assisting and even directing him. He communicated with them by means of typtology, and having remarked that these mysterious operators did not seem fully to understand the scientific interest of the phenomena, he questioned them, and concluded from their replies that they were only laborers of some sort, manipulating forces which they did not understand, and accomplishing a task required of them by a higher order of beings who could not or did not condescend to do the work themselves.

The Great Secret

It may of course be maintained that these invisible collaborators emanate from the subconsciousness of the medium or of other persons present, so that the problem is still unsolved. But a conviction which a scientist who was, to begin with, as skeptical as Dr. Crawford, was gradually, and by the very force of things, led to accept, deserves to be seriously considered. In any case his experiments, like those in connection with the odic fluid, prove once more that our being is far more immaterial, more psychic, more mysterious, more powerful, and assuredly more enduring than we believe it to be; and this was taught us by the primitive religions, as it is taught by the occultists who have been inspired thereby.

19

While we do not lose sight of the other spiritualistic manifestations—the posthumous apparitions, the phenomena of psychometry and materialization, the provision of the future, the mystery of speaking animals, the miracles of Lourdes and other places of pilgrimage, which we mention here only to show that we have not overlooked them,—here, as compared with the prodigious and arrogant affirmations of the past, are the half-certainties, the petty details slowly reconquered by the occultists of to-day. At first sight this is little

enough, and even if the great central problem
of our metapsychics, the problem of survival,
were at length solved, this long and eagerly
anticipated solution would not take us very far;
assuredly not nearly so far as the priests of India and Egypt went. But modest though they
may be, the discoveries of our occultists have
at least the advantage of being founded upon
facts which we can verify, and should therefore
be of far greater value to us than the more impressive hypotheses which have hitherto evaded
verification.

20

Now it is quite possible that to penetrate
any further into the regions which they are ex-
ploring, the experimental methods which are
the safest in other sciences may prove insuffi-
cient. Other elements must be considered
than those which science is accustomed to encounter. Forces may perhaps be in question
of a more spiritual nature than those of our
intellect, and in order to grasp and control them
it may first be necessary to apply ourselves to
our own spiritualization. It is an advantage
to possess perfectly organized laboratories, but
the true laboratory whence the ultimate discoveries will proceed is probably within us.
This the priests and Magi of the great religions seem to have understood better than we,

for when they purposed to enter the ultra-spiritual domains of nature they underwent a protracted preparation. They felt that it was not enough that they should be learned, but that they must before all become saints. They began by the training of their will, by the sacrifice of their whole being, by dying to all desire. They enfolded their intellectual energies in a moral force which led them far more directly to the plane on which the strange phenomena which they were investigating had their being. It is probable enough that there are in the invisible, or the infinite, things that the understanding cannot grasp, on which it has no hold, but to which another faculty can attain; and this faculty is perhaps what is known as the soul, or that higher subconsciousness which the ancient religions had learned to cultivate by spiritual exercises, and above all by a renunciation and a spiritual concentration of which we have forgotten the rules and even the idea.

CHAPTER XII

CONCLUSIONS

I

WE have already, in the course of this inquiry, become familiar with most of the conclusions to be drawn therefrom, and it will therefore suffice to recall the most important in a brief recapitulation.

At the very beginning of the old religions, and especially at the beginning of that which seems to be the most ancient of all and the source of all the rest, there is no secret doctrine and no revelation; there is only the prehistoric tradition of a metaphysics which we should to-day call purely rationalistic. The confession of absolute ignorance as regards the nature, attributes, character, purposes, and existence even of the First Cause or the God of Gods is public and explicit. It is a vast negation; we know nothing, we can know nothing, we never shall know anything, for it may be that God Himself does not know everything.

This unknown First Cause is of necessity infinite, for the infinite alone is unknowable, and the God of Gods would no longer be the God of Gods, and could not understand Himself, unless He were all things. His infinity inevitably gives rise to pantheism; for if the First Cause is everything, everything partakes in the First Cause, and it is not possible to imagine anything that can set bounds to it and is not the Cause itself, or part of the Cause, or does not proceed from the Cause. From this pantheism proceeds in its turn the belief in immortality and the ultimate optimism, for, the Cause being infinite in space and time, nothing that is of it or in it can be destroyed without destroying a part of the Cause itself; which is impossible, since it would still be the nothingness that sought to circumscribe it, just as nothing could be eternally unhappy without condemning part of itself to eternal unhappiness.

Absolute agnosticism, with its consequences; the infinity of the divine, pantheism, universal immortality, and ultimate optimism—here is the point of departure of the great primitive teachers, pure intellects, and implacable logicians, such as were the mysterious Atlanteans, if we may believe the traditions of the occultists; and would not the very same point of departure impose itself to-day upon those who should seek to found a new religion which would not be repugnant to the ever-increasing exactions of human reason?

Conclusions

2

But if all is God and necessarily immortal, it is none the less certain that men and things and worlds disappear. From this moment we bid good-by to the logical consequences of the great confession of ignorance to enter the labyrinth of theories which are no longer unassailable, and which, for that matter, are not at the outset put before us as revelations but as mere metaphysical hypotheses, as speculations of great antiquity, born of the necessity of reconciling the facts with the too abstract and too rigid deductions of human reason.

As a matter of fact, according to these hypotheses man, the world and the universe do not perish; they disappear and reappear alternately throughout eternity, in virtue of Maya, the illusion of ignorance. When they no longer exist for us or for any one, they still exist virtually, where no one sees them; and those who have ceased to see them do not cease to exist as though they saw them. Similarly, when God sets bounds to Himself, in order to manifest Himself and to become conscious of a portion of Himself, He does not cease to be infinite and unknowable to Himself. He seems for a moment to place Himself at the point of view or within the comprehension of those whom He has quickened in His bosom.

The Great Secret

This last hypothesis must in the beginning have been, as it is at present and always will be, a mere makeshift; but there was a time when it became a sort of dogma which, eagerly welcomed by the imagination, soon completely replaced the great primitive negation. From that moment, despairing of knowing the unknowable, man duplicated and subdivided and multiplied it, relegating the inconceivable First Cause to the inaccessible Infinite, and henceforth concerned himself only with those secondary causes by which it manifests itself and acts.

He does not ask himself, or rather he does not dare to ask, how, the First Cause being essentially unknowable, its manifestations could be considered as known, although it had not ceased to be unknowable; and we enter the vast vicious circle in which mankind must resign itself to live under penalty of condemning itself to an eternal negation, an eternal immobility and ignorance and silence.

Unable to know God in Himself, man contents himself with seeking and questioning Him in His creatures, and above all in mankind. He thought to find Him there, and the religions were born, with their gods, their cults, their sacrifices, their beliefs, their moralities, their hells and heavens. The relationship which binds them all to the unknown Cause is

more and more forgotten, reappearing only at
certain moments, as it reappeared, for example, long afterwards, in Buddhism, in the meta-
physicians, in the ancient mysteries and occult
traditions. But despite this oblivion, and
thanks to the idea of this First Cause, necessarily one, invisible, intangible, and inconceivable, which we are consequently compelled to
regard as purely spiritual; two of the great
principles of the primitive religion, which subsequently permeated those religions which
sprang from it, have survived, deep-rooted and
tenacious of life, secretly repeating, beneath all
outward appearances, that the essence of all
things is one and that the spirit is the source
of all, the only certitude, the sole eternal reality.

3

From these two principles, which at bottom
are only one, proceeds all that primitive ethic
which became the great ethic of humanity: unity being the ideal and sovereign good, evil
means separation, division, and multiplicity,
and matter is finally but one result of separation or multiplicity. To return to unity, therefore, we must strip ourselves, must escape from
matter, which is but an inferior form or degradation of the spirit.

It was thus that man found, or believed that

he had found, the purpose of the unknowable, and the key of all morality without, however, venturing to ask himself why this rupture of unity and this degradation of the spirit had been necessary; as though we had supposed that the First Cause, which might have kept all things in the state of unity, in its undivided, immobile, and supremely blessed bosom, had been condemned, by a superior and irresistible law, to movement and eternal recommencement.

These ideas, too purely metaphysical to nourish a religion, were soon in India itself covered by a prodigious vegetation of myths, and gradually became the secret of the Brahmans, who cultivated them, developed them, gave them profundity, and complicated them, to the verge of insanity. Thence they spread over the face of the earth, or returned to the place whence they had set forth; for while it is permissible to attempt the chronological localization of a central source, it is impossible for us to determine where they rose to the surface in the ages before the dawn of history, unless we refer to the theosophical legends of the Seven Races, which we might perhaps accept if we were supplied with documents less open to criticism than those which have hitherto been offered to us.

Conclusions

4

At all events, it is easy enough to follow the progress of these ideas through the world known to history; whether they went hand in hand, or one following another, through India, Egypt, and Persia; or found their way into Chaldea and pre-Socratic Greece by means of myths or contacts or migrations unknown to us; or, especially in the case of Hellas, through the Orphic poems, collected during the Alexandrian period, but dating from legendary ages, and containing lines which, as Émile Burnouf observes in his *Science des Religions,* are translated word for word from the Vedic hymns.[1]

As a result of the Egyptian bondage, the Babylonian captivity, and the conquest of Cyrus, they reached the Bible, changing their shape to harmonize with the Jewish monotheism; but in secret they were preserved, almost undefiled, by oral transmission, in the cabala, in which the En-Sof, as we have seen, is the exact reproduction of the Hindu Unknowable, and leads to an almost similar agnosticism, pantheism, optimism, and ethic.

These ideas, stifled beneath the Bible in the Jewish world, and in the Greco-Roman world

[1] Émile Burnouf, *La Science des Religions;* p. 105.

beneath the weight of the official religions and philosophies, survived among the secret sects, and notably among the Essenes, and also in the mysteries; reappearing in the light of day about the beginning of the Christian era, in the Gnostic and Neoplatonic schools of philosophy, and later on in the cabala, when they were finally put into writing; whence they passed, more or less distorted, into the occultism of the middle ages, of which they constitute the sole foundation.

5

We see, accordingly, that occultism, or rather the secret doctrine, variable in its forms, often extremely obscure, above all during the middle ages, but almost everywhere identical as to its basis, was always a protest of the human reason, faithful to its prehistoric traditions, against the arbitrary assertions and pretended revelations of the public and official religions. To their baseless dogmas, their anthropomorphical manifestations of the divine, illogical, petty, and unacceptable, they opposed the confession of an absolute and invincible ignorance of all essential points. From this confession, which at first sight seems to destroy everything, but which leads, almost of necessity, to a spiritualistic conception of the universe; it was able to derive a metaphysics, a mysticism, and a morality much purer, loftier, more disinterested, and above all more rational than those which were born of the religions which were stifling it. One might even prove that all that these religions still have in common on the heights where all are united—all that could not be debased to the level of the material requirements of an over-long life—all that is to be found in them that is awe-inspiring, infinite, imperishable, and universal—they owe to that immemorial metaphysic into which they struck their first roots.

It would even seem that in proportion as time removes them from this metaphysic the spirit leads them back to it; thus, to value only the two latest religions, without mention of all that they borrowed from it more directly, we find that the God the Father of Christianity and the Allah of Islam are much nearer to the En-Sof of the cabala than to the Jahweh of the Bible; and that the Word of St. John, which is not mentioned in the Old Testament or the synoptics, is merely the Logos of the Gnostics and the Neoplatonists, who themselves obtained it from India and Egypt.

6

Is this, then, the great secret of humanity, which has been hidden with such care beneath mysterious and sacred formulæ, beneath rites

which were sometimes terrifying, beneath
formidable reticences and silences: an unmiti-
gated negation, a stupendous void, a hopeless
ignorance? Yes, it is only this: and it is as
well that it is nothing else; for a God and a
universe small enough for the little brain of
man to circumnavigate them, to understand
their nature and their economy, to discover
their origin, their aims and their limits, would
be so pitiful and so restricted that no one would
resign himself to remain eternally as their
prisoner. Humanity has need of the infinite,
with its corollary of invincible ignorance, if it
is not to feel itself the dupe or victim of an
unforgivable experiment or a blunder impossible of evasion. There was no need to call
it into existence, but since it has been raised
out of nothingness it must needs enjoy the
boundlessness of space and time of which it
has been vouchsafed the conception. It has
the right to participate in all that has given it
life, before it can forgive it for bringing it
into the world. And it is not able thus to
participate save on the condition that it cannot understand it. Every certainty—at all
events, until our minds are liberated from the
chains that fetter them—would become an
enclosing wall on which all desire to live would
be shattered. Let us therefore rejoice that
we know of no further certainties beyond an

ignorance as infinite as the world or the God Who is its subject.

7

After so many efforts, so many experiments, we find ourselves precisely at the point from which our great teachers set out. They bequeathed to us a wisdom which we are hardly beginning to clear of the rubbish that the centuries have left upon it; and beneath this rubbish we find intact the proudest confession of ignorance that man has ever ventured to pronounce. To a lover of illusion this means but little; to a lover of truth it is much indeed. We know at last that there has never been any ultra-human revelation, any direct and irrecusable message from divinity, no ineffable secret; and that all man believes himself to know of God, of His origin and His ends, he has drawn from his own powers of reason. Before we had interrogated our prehistoric ancestors we more than suspected that all revelations, in the sense of the word understood by the religious, were and will always be impossible; for we cannot reveal to any one more than he is capable of understanding, and God alone can understand God. But it was easy to imagine that having, so to speak, been witnesses of the birth of the world, they ought to know more of it than we do, since they were still nearer to God. But they were not nearer to God; they were simply nearer to the human reason, which had not as yet been obscured by the inventions of thousands of years. They are content with giving us the only landmarks which this reason has been able to discover in the unknowable: pantheism, spiritualism, immortality, and final optimism; confiding the rest to the hypotheses of their successors, and wisely leaving unanswered, as we should leave them to-day, all those insoluble problems which the succeeding religions blindly attacked, often in an ingenious manner which was none the less always arbitrary and sometimes childish.

8

Need we again recapitulate these problems? —the passage from the virtual to the actual; from being to becoming; from non-existence to existence; and the descent of the spirit into matter—that is, the origin of evil and the ascent from matter to spirit; the necessity of emerging from a state of eternal bliss, to return thither after purification and ordeals whose indispensable nature is beyond our comprehension; eternal recommencements, to reach a goal which has always fled us, since it has never been attained, although in the past men had as much leisure to attain it as they will ever have in the future.

Conclusions

I might increase beyond all measures this balance-sheet of the unknowable. To close the account it is enough to add that the question which rightly or wrongly causes us the greatest anxiety—that which concerns the fate of our consciousness and our personality when absorbed by the divine, is likewise unanswered, for Nirvana determines nothing and specifies nothing, and the Buddha, the last interpreter of the great esoteric doctrines, himself confesses that he does not know whether this absorption is absorption into nothingness or into eternal blessedness. "The Sublime has not revealed it to him."

"The Sublime has not revealed it to him"; for nothing has been revealed and nothing has been solved, because it is probable that nothing will ever be capable of solution, and because it is possible that beings whose intellect must be a million times more powerful than our own would still be unable to discover a solution. To understand the Creation, to tell us whence it comes and whither it goes, one would have to be its author; and even then, asks the "Rig-Veda," at the very source of primordial wisdom: "and even then, does He know it?"

The Great Secret, the only secret, is that all things are secret. Let us at least learn, in the school of our mysterious ancestors, to make allowance, as they did, for the unknowable,

267

The Great Secret

and to search only for what is there: that is, the certainty that all things are God, that all things exist in Him and should end in happiness, and that the only divinity which we can hope to understand is to be found in the depths of our own souls. The Great Secret has not changed its aspect; it remains where and what it was for our forebears. At the very beginning they managed to derive from the unknowable the purest morality which we have known, and since we now find ourselves at the same point of the unknowable, it would be dangerous, not to say impossible, to deduce other lessons therefrom. And these doctrines, of which the nobler portions have remained the same, and which differ only in their baser characteristics, in all the religions whose various dogmas are at bottom only mythological translations or interpretations of these too abstract truths, would have made man something that as yet he is not, had he but had the courage to follow them. Do not let us forget them: this is the last and the best counsel of the mystical testament whose pages we have just been turning over.